Maths Progress

Purposeful Practice Book

Series Editors:

Dr Naomi Norman and Katherine Pate

◆ Skills practice ◆ Problem-solving practice

2

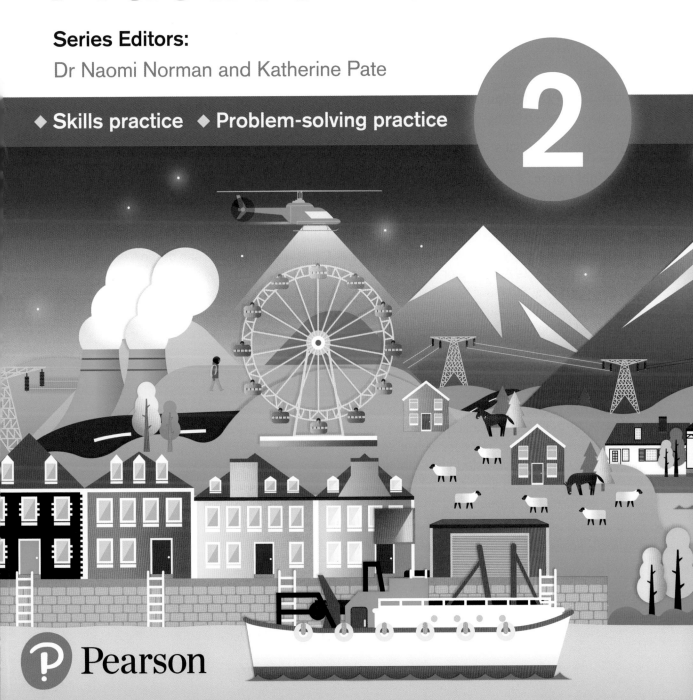

P Pearson

Published by Pearson Education Limited, 80 Strand, London, WC2R 0RL.

www.pearsonschoolsandcolleges.co.uk

Text © Pearson Education Limited 2019
Edited by Haremi Ltd.
Typeset by York Publishing Solutions Pvt. Ltd.
Cover design by Pearson Education Limited 2018
Cover illustration by Robert Samuel Hanson
Index compiled by LNS Indexing

The rights of Dr Naomi Norman, Diane Oliver and Katherine Pate to be identified as authors of this work have been asserted by them in accordance with the Copyright, Designs and Patents Act 1988.

First published 2019

23
10 9 8

British Library Cataloguing in Publication Data
A catalogue record for this book is available from the British Library

ISBN 978 1 292 27998 5

Printed in Great Britain by Bell and Bain Ltd, Glasgow

Note from the publisher
Pearson has robust editorial processes, including answer and fact checks, to ensure the accuracy of the content in this publication, and every effort is made to ensure this publication is free of errors. We are, however, only human, and occasionally errors do occur. Pearson is not liable for any misunderstandings that arise as a result of errors in this publication, but it is our priority to ensure that the content is accurate. If you spot an error, please do contact us at resourcescorrections@pearson.com so we can make sure it is corrected.

Contents

Maths Progress
Purposeful Practice Book 2

8 key messages from Series Editors Dr Naomi Norman and Katherine Pate

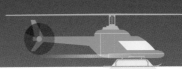

These Maths Progress Purposeful Practice books offer:

1 Lots of practice – you can never have too much!

2 Practice that develops mathematical confidence.

3 Purposeful practice questions that lead students on a path to understanding. These questions:
   - cannot be answered mechanically, by rote
   - make connections to prior knowledge
   - develop thinking skills
   - target specific concepts

4 Reflect and reason questions to:
   - make students aware of their understanding
   - show teachers what students do (or don't yet!) understand
   - encourage students to think about the underlying mathematical patterns

5 Problem-solving practice to:
   - allow students to apply their understanding to problem-solving questions and contexts
   - practices problem-solving strategies
   - lay the groundwork for GCSE exams

6 Embed the key skills and build confidence to succeed at KS3 by supporting the new Maths Progress (Second Edition), preparing students for their GCSEs.

7 Designed with the help of UK teachers so you can use them flexibly alongside your current resources, in class or for independent study.

8 Purposeful practice and problem-solving practice all in one book – the first of its kind.

Get to know your Purposeful Practice Book

Key points

Key points to remind students what they need to know.

△ Purposeful practice

The Purposeful Practice Books start with short practice questions, carefully crafted to lead students on a path to understanding the mathematics.

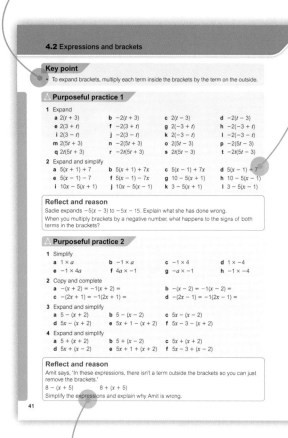

4.2 Expressions and brackets

Key point
• To expand brackets, multiply each term inside the brackets by the term on the outside.

△ **Purposeful practice 1**

1 Expand
a $2(t + 3)$　b $-2(t + 3)$　c $2(t - 3)$　d $-2(t - 3)$
e $2(3 + t)$　f $-2(3 + t)$　g $2(-3 + t)$　h $-2(-3 + t)$
i $2(3 - t)$　j $-2(3 - t)$　k $2(-3 - t)$　l $-2(-3 - t)$
m $2(5t + 3)$　n $-2(5t + 3)$　o $2(5t - 3)$　p $-2(5t - 3)$
q $2t(5t + 3)$　r $-2t(5t + 3)$　s $2t(5t - 3)$　t $-2t(5t - 3)$

2 Expand and simplify
a $5(x + 1) + 7$　b $5(x + 1) + 7x$　c $5(x - 1) + 7x$　d $5(x - 1) + 7$
e $5(x - 1) - 7$　f $5(x - 1) - 7x$　g $10 - 5(x + 1)$　h $10 - 5(x - 1)$
i $10x - 5(x + 1)$　j $10x - 5(x - 1)$　k $3 - 5(x + 1)$　l $3 - 5(x - 1)$

Reflect and reason
Sadie expands $-5(x - 3)$ to $-5x - 15$. Explain what she has done wrong.
When you multiply brackets by a negative number, what happens to the signs of both terms in the brackets?

△ **Purposeful practice 2**

1 Simplify
a $1 \times a$　b $-1 \times a$　c -1×4　d 1×-4
e $-1 \times 4a$　f $4a \times -1$　g $-a \times -1$　h -1×-4

2 Copy and complete
a $-(x + 2) = -1(x + 2) =$　b $-(x - 2) = -1(x - 2) =$
c $-(2x + 1) = -1(2x + 1) =$　d $-(2x - 1) = -1(2x - 1) =$

3 Expand and simplify
a $5 - (x + 2)$　b $5 - (x - 2)$　c $5x - (x - 2)$
d $5x - (x + 2)$　e $5x + 1 - (x + 2)$　f $5x - 3 - (x + 2)$

4 Expand and simplify
a $5 + (x + 2)$　b $5 + (x - 2)$　c $5x + (x + 2)$
d $5x + (x - 2)$　e $5x + 1 + (x + 2)$　f $5x - 3 + (x - 2)$

Reflect and reason
Amit says, 'In these expressions, there isn't a term outside the brackets so you can just remove the brackets.'
$8 - (x + 5)$　$8 + (x + 5)$
Simplify the expressions and explain why Amit is wrong.

41

⊠ **Problem-solving practice**

1 Match each expression for the area of a rectangle with the correct rectangle.
a $12x + 6$　b $12x + 8$　c $12x + 10$　d $12x + 9$

2 Copy and complete.
a $-3(a \square \square) = \square + 6$　b $-2(-5b \square \square) = \square + 14$

3 A question on expanding brackets gives the answer $4x - 8$.
What could the question have been?
Find as many different answers as you can.

4 In this algebra wheel, the opposite terms multiply to give the expression in the centre.
Copy and complete the algebra wheel.

5 An expression for the area of the rectangle is $15m^2 - 10m$.
The length of the rectangle is $3m - 2$.
What is the width of the rectangle?

width

$3m - 2$

6 Match these expressions into equivalent pairs.
$2(x - 3) + 7$　$2(x - 4) + 7$　$7 - (-2x + 3)$　$7 + (-2x + 4)$　$7 - (2x + 3)$
$7 - (-2x - 3)$　$-2x + 11$　$2x - 1$　$2x + 10$　$-2x + 4$　$2x + 1$

7 Alice and Helen are asked to expand $4x - 5 - (x - 3)$.
Alice writes
$4x - 5 - (x - 3) = 4x - 5 - x + 3$
$= 3x - 8$
Helen writes
$4x - 5 - (x - 3) = 4x - 5 - x - 3$
$= 3x - 8$
Both Alice and Helen are incorrect.
a Explain what Alice has done wrong.
b Explain Helen's mistake.
c Write the correct answer.

Unit 4 Expressions and brackets　42

Reflect and reason

Thought provoking questions that encourage students to articulate a mathematical pattern, structure or relationship.

⊠ Problem-solving practice

These questions lead on from Purposeful practice, allowing students to apply the skills they have learnt in different contexts where the steps aren't obvious and they must apply different strategies.

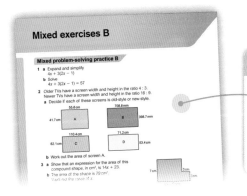

Mixed exercises B

Mixed problem-solving practice B

1 a Expand and simplify
$4x + 3(2x - 1)$
b Solve
$4x + 3(2x - 1) = 57$
2 Older TVs have a screen width and height in the ratio 4 : 3.
Newer TVs have a screen width and height in the ratio 16 : 9.
a Decide if each of these screens is old-style or new-style.

b Work out the area of screen A.
3 a Show that an expression for the area of this compound shape, in cm², is $14x + 23$.
b The area of the shape is 79 cm².
Work out the value of x.

Mixed exercises

There are Mixed exercise pages in the book, where students can bring topics together to encourage them to make links between the mathematical concepts they have studied previously. This is to ensure that the mathematical concepts are not learnt in isolation.

How Purposeful Practice builds the skills to succeed:

△ Purposeful practice has been embedded in 3 different ways:

1. **Variation**

   Carefully crafted questions that are minimally varied throughout an exercise.
   As students work out the answers, they are exposed to what stays the same and what
   changes, from question to question. In doing so, by the end of the exercise, students
   deepen their understanding of the mathematical patterns, structures and relationships
   that underlie concepts.

2. **Variation and progression**

   A mixture of minimally varied questions, along with small-stepped questions that get
   incrementally harder. These exercises are designed to both deepen understanding
   and move students on.

3. **Progression**

   Questions where the skills required become incrementally harder. These small-
   stepped questions mean there are no uncomfortable jumps, and help to build
   students' confidence.

Reflect and reason

Metacognition (reflection) is a powerful tool that is used to help students become aware
of their own understanding. Reasoning is a key part of the GCSE (9–1), so we've included
lots of opportunities for students to show what they do (or don't yet!) understand.

⊠ Problem-solving practice is where the skill(s) from each sub-unit can be
demonstrated and applied. These problem-solving activities will be a mixture of
contextualised problems, 'working backwards' problems, and synoptic problems, ensuring
that the skills practised in each sub-unit are fully embedded in new and interesting ways to
build confidence.

Maths Progress Second Edition

These KS3 Purposeful Practice Books are part of *Maths Progress Second Edition*.

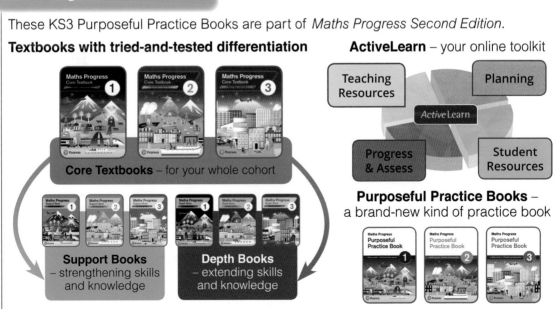

Textbooks with tried-and-tested differentiation

Core Textbooks – for your whole cohort

Support Books – strengthening skills and knowledge

Depth Books – extending skills and knowledge

ActiveLearn – your online toolkit

Teaching Resources

Planning

*Active*Learn

Progress & Assess

Student Resources

Purposeful Practice Books – a brand-new kind of practice book

For more information go to www.pearsonschools.co.uk

1 Number

Key points

- Doubling and halving is a mental strategy for multiplication. You double one number and halve the other to make the calculation easier.
- Rounding and adjusting is a mental strategy for multiplication. Round one number to a multiple of 10 to make the multiplication easier. Then adjust by adding or subtracting.
- The column method is a written strategy for calculations.

△ Purposeful practice 1

Use the doubling and halving strategy to work out

1 a 16×5 **b** 22×5 **c** 48×5 **d** 5×86 **e** 34×5 **f** 5×92

2 a 14×50 **b** 26×50 **c** 50×42 **d** 50×88 **e** 52×50 **f** 50×74

3 a 1.5×18 **b** 2.5×18 **c** 18×3.5 **d** 18×4.5 **e** 5.5×18

4 a 2.2×1.5 **b** 2.2×2.5 **c** 2.2×3.5 **d** 4.5×2.2

Reflect and reason

Which decimal did you double and which did you halve in **Q4a**? Explain why.

△ Purposeful practice 2

Use the rounding and adjusting strategy to work out

1 a 2×101 **b** 2×102 **c** 2×103 **d** 2×99 **e** 2×98 **f** 2×97

2 a 3×101 **b** 3×102 **c** 3×103 **d** 3×99 **e** 3×98 **f** 3×97

3 a 3×19 **b** 3×29 **c** 4×19 **d** 4×29 **e** 6×49 **f** 6×59

4 a 7×1001 **b** 8×1001 **c** 7×999 **d** 8×999 **e** 1001×9 **f** 999×9

Reflect and reason

How do you decide whether to add or subtract when adjusting?

△ Purposeful practice 3

Estimate the answers to these calculations, then use the column method to work out the correct answers.

1 a $3621 + 274$ **b** $3621 + 274 - 743$

  c $4785 - 364$ **d** $4785 - 364 - 211$

  e $6317 + 459$ **f** $6317 + 459 - 93$

  g $7295 + 836 - 724$ **h** $5623 - 471 - 328$

2 a $25.4 + 3.07$

   c $41.9 - 13.8$

   e $65.3 - 28.71 + 8.92$

   b $25.4 + 3.07 - 7.12$

   d $41.9 - 13.8 - 6.03$

   f $25.4 + 3.07 - 6.29 - 1.07$

Reflect and reason

Alice works out **Q1g** like this.

Does Alice still get the correct answer? Explain why.

Do you think Alice's method is easier or harder than working out $7295 + 836$ and then subtracting 724? Explain why.

$$
\begin{array}{r}
8\ 3\ 6 \\
-\ 7\ 2\ 4 \\
\hline
1\ 1\ 2
\end{array}
\qquad
\begin{array}{r}
7\ 2\ 9\ 5 \\
+\ \ \ 1\ 1\ 2 \\
\hline
\end{array}
$$

⊠ Problem-solving practice

1 Match each multiplication in the first box with an equivalent multiplication in the second box.

| 3.5×86 | 14×25 | 28×25 | 14×43 | 4.5×86 | 18×43 |

| 14×50 | 9×86 | 7×43 | 9×43 | 7×50 | 7×86 |

2 Ben uses the doubling and halving strategy to work out 50×36.
He writes

$$
\begin{aligned}
50 \times 36 &= 25 \times 72 \\
&= 20 \times 72 + 5 \times 72 \\
&= 1440 + 360 = 1800
\end{aligned}
$$

How could Ben have made this calculation easier?

3 Using the doubling and halving strategy gives 11×70.
What might the calculation have been before the strategy was used?
Write both possible calculations.

4 Abi, Becky and Cathy work out 8×79.

Abi writes
$8 \times 80 = 640$
$640 - 79 = 561$
So $8 \times 79 = 561$

Becky writes
$8 \times 80 = 640$
$640 + 8 = 648$
So $8 \times 79 = 648$

Cathy writes
$8 \times 80 = 640$
$640 - 8 = 632$
So $8 \times 79 = 632$

Who is correct? Explain why.
Explain what mistakes the others made.

5 Copy and complete each calculation.

   a $7 \times \square = 7 \times 60 + 7$

   c $\square \times \square = 8 \times 100 - 24$

   b $12 \times \square = 12 \times 40 - 24$

   d $\square \times \square = 11 \times 200 + 33$

6 Henry walks to his friend's house. After 1.4 km, he stops at a shop. He then continues for 0.78 km to his friend's house.
How far has he walked in total?

7 Jayesh is asked to work out $54.3 + 2.87 + 96.1$.
Jayesh's answer is 179.1 and his working is shown.
Is Jayesh correct? Explain why.

$$
\begin{array}{r}
5\ 4.3 \\
2.8\ 7 \\
+\ \ 9\ 6.1 \\
\hline
17\ 9.1 \\
{\scriptstyle 1\ \ 1}
\end{array}
$$

8 Ava has a 4.5 m long plank.
She cuts 1.75 m and then another 1.68 m off the plank.
What is the length of the remaining plank?

Key points

- When you divide an integer (a whole number) by a second integer and there is no remainder, then the first integer is said to be divisible by the second integer, for example, 48 ÷ 4 = 12 so 48 is divisible by 4.
- A number is divisible by 2 if it ends in an even digit.
  A number is divisible by 3 if the sum of its digits is divisible by 3.
  A number is divisible by 4 if its last two digits are divisible by 4.
- A zero on the end of an integer increases its value by ×10.
  A zero on the end of a decimal number does not change its value. For example,
  782: put a zero on the end and it becomes 7820.
  782.1: put a zero on the end and it becomes 782.10 (that is, the same number).

△ Purposeful practice 1

1 | 42   387   428   504   672   846   1064   3462 |
  Write all the numbers in this box that are divisible by
  a 2   **b** 3   **c** 4   **d** 2 and 3   **e** 3 and 4

2 Write a number that is divisible by 2 and 3, and has
  a 2 digits   **b** 3 digits   **c** 4 digits

3 Write a number that is divisible by 3 and 4, and has
  a 2 digits   **b** 3 digits   **c** 4 digits

Reflect and reason

Explain why a number is divisible by 6 if it is divisible by 2 and 3. Give examples.
Explain why a number is divisible by 12 if it is divisible by 3 and 4. Give examples.

△ Purposeful practice 2

1 Copy and complete these divisions.

   a £508.20 ÷ 12

$$\begin{array}{r} 42.\square\square \\ 12\overline{)£508.20} \\ \underline{48}\!\downarrow \\ 28 \\ \underline{24}\downarrow \\ 42 \end{array}$$

   b £391.80 ÷ 12

$$12\overline{)£391.80}$$

   c 782.1 ÷ 15

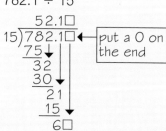

   d 512.4 ÷ 15

$$15\overline{)512.4}$$

2 Work out

    a $921.6 \div 12$ **b** $9892.8 \div 12$ **c** $4147.5 \div 15$

    d $65.4 \div 12$ **e** $401.1 \div 15$ **f** $890.4 \div 16$

Reflect and reason

Look at your working for **Q2**.

When do you put a zero at the end of a decimal when doing written division?

◻ Problem-solving practice

1 Ruth says, '16 872 is divisible by 2, 3, 4, 6 and 12.'
Is Ruth correct? Explain how you know.

2 Copy and complete each statement with a missing digit.
Where there is more than one answer write all the possible answers.

    a 3☐5 is divisible by 3.   **b** 451☐ is divisible by 2.

    c 314☐ is divisible by 4.   **d** 241☐ is divisible by 2 and 3.

3 List the numbers from 1 to 12 that 83 520 is divisible by.

4 Write a 4-digit number that is divisible by 2, 3 and 4.

5 Some of the numbers in the calculation have been smudged.
Copy and complete the calculation.

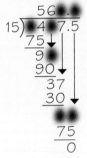

6 Riya works out $1829.1 \div 12$. She writes

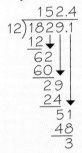

So $1829.1 \div 12 = 152.4$ remainder 3.

    a Explain why Riya's calculation will be marked wrong.

    b Work out $1829.1 \div 12$. You must show your working.

7 Chris buys a car costing £9075.
He borrows the money from his parents.
He pays them back in equal payments each month over a year.
How much does Chris pay his parents each month to pay for the car?

Key points

- Adding a negative number $(+ -)$ or subtracting a positive number $(- +)$ is the same as subtracting $(-)$, for example, $2 + -3 = 2 - +3 = 2 - 3 = -1$.
- Subtracting a negative number $(- -)$ is the same as adding, for example, $2 - -3 = 2 + 3 = 5$
- positive $\times$ positive = positive   positive $\times$ negative = negative
  negative $\times$ negative = positive   negative $\times$ positive = negative

△ Purposeful practice 1

1 Work out

   a $5 + 1$ **b** $5 + 0$ **c** $5 + -1$ **d** $5 + -2$

   e $5 + -3$ **f** $5 + -4$ **g** $5 + -5$ **h** $5 + -6$

2 Work out

   a $5 - -1$ **b** $5 - -2$ **c** $5 - -3$ **d** $5 - -4$

   e $5 - -5$ **f** $5 - -6$ **g** $5 - -7$ **h** $5 - -8$

3 Write all the calculations A–H that give an answer of

   a 15

   b -15

   c neither 15 nor -15

A: $5 + -10$ B: $5 - +10$ C: $-5 - +10$ D: $-5 + -10$

E: $5 - -10$ F: $10 - -5$ G: $-5 - -10$ H: $-10 - -5$

Reflect and reason

When there are two signs between numbers, does it matter which sign is first?

△ Purposeful practice 2

1 Work out

   a 4×5 **b** -4×-5 **c** -4×5 **d** 4×-5

2 Work out

   a $32 \div 4$ **b** $32 \div -4$ **c** $-32 \div 4$ **d** $-32 \div -4$

3 Write all the calculations A–H that give an answer of

   a 12

   b -12

   c neither 12 nor -12

A: 12×-1 B: -2×6 C: -2×-6 D: 3×-4

E: $36 \div -3$ F: $-36 \div -4$ G: $-24 \div -2$ H: $24 \div -2$

Reflect and reason

Anna says, '-2×-2 and $2 - -2$ have the same answer.' Is she correct? Explain.

Billy says, '-3×-3 and $3 - -3$ also have the same answer.' Is he correct? Explain.

1 a Charlie writes

$-7 - -7 = -14$

Is Charlie correct? Explain why.

b Ewan writes

$10 + -6 = 10 - 6$

Is Ewan correct? Explain your answer.

2 Tess has stuck stars over some of the numbers in her work.
Write each number that Tess has covered.

a $2 + ☆ = -7$ **b** $☆ - 5 = -3$ **c** $12 + ☆ = -20$
d $-6 + ☆ = -15$ **e** $☆ + 8 = 1$ **f** $-15 + ☆ = 4$

3 Copy and complete these calculations.

a $\square - \square = 1$ **b** $\square - \square = -4$ **c** $\square - \square = -10$
d $\square + \square = 0$ **e** $\square + \square = -3$ **f** $\square + \square = -20$

4 Georgie is thinking of two different negative numbers.
The total of her two numbers is -50.
What two numbers may Georgie be thinking of?

5 In a magic square every row, column and the two diagonals have
the same total.
Copy and complete the magic square.

−3	2	1
	0	

6 Josh draws this multiplication grid.
Is Josh correct? Explain.

×	2	1	0	−1	−2
2	4	2	0	−2	−4
1	2	1	0	−1	−2
0	0	0	0	0	0
−1	−2	−1	0	−1	−2
−2	−4	−2	0	−2	−4

7 Copy and complete these calculations.

a $6 \times \square = -42$ **b** $\square \times -8 = 40$ **c** $-56 \div \square = -8$
d $\square \div -4 = 9$ **e** $\square \div -12 = -8$ **f** $-9 \times \square = -36$

8 Copy and complete the multiplication grid.

×		7		
−2	6			
	15	−35		
6			−48	
9				99

9 What two integers multiply to give an answer of -9?
Write all the possible combinations.

Key points

- $2^3 = 2 \times 2 \times 2$
  2^3 is '2 cubed' or '2 to the power 3'.
- Finding the cube root is the inverse of finding the cube of a number.
  3 cubed is 27, so the cube root of $27 = \sqrt[3]{27} = 3$.
- $3^2 = 9$ and $(-3)^2 = 9$
  The positive square root of 9 is 3. The negative square root of 9 is -3. So $\sqrt{9} = \pm 3$.
  The $\sqrt{9}$ symbol is used for the principal square root, which is always a positive number.
  For example, $\sqrt{9} = 3$
- Priority of operations: BIDMAS
  Brackets
  Indices (powers and roots)
  Division and Multiplication
  Addition and Subtraction

△ Purposeful practice 1

1 Work out

  a $(-1)^2$ **b** $(-2)^2$ **c** $(-3)^2$ **d** $(-4)^2$

  e $(-5)^2$ **f** $(-6)^2$ **g** $(-7)^2$ **h** $(-8)^2$

  i $(-9)^2$ **j** $(-10)^2$ **k** $(-11)^2$ **l** $(-12)^2$

2 Write the positive and negative square roots of these numbers.

  a $\sqrt{9}$ **b** $\sqrt{36}$ **c** $\sqrt{144}$ **d** $\sqrt{1}$

  e $\sqrt{16}$ **f** $\sqrt{100}$ **g** $\sqrt{4}$ **h** $\sqrt{121}$

  i $\sqrt{64}$ **j** $\sqrt{25}$ **k** $\sqrt{49}$ **l** $\sqrt{81}$

Reflect and reason

Katrina says, '$(-20)^2$ is 40, and so $\sqrt{40}$ is 20 or -20.'
What mistake has she made?

△ Purposeful practice 2

1 Work out

  a 1^3 **b** $(-1)^3$ **c** 2^3 **d** $(-2)^3$

  e 3^3 **f** $(-3)^3$ **g** 4^3 **h** $(-4)^3$

  i 5^3 **j** $(-5)^3$ **k** 10^3 **l** $(-10)^3$

2 Work out

  a $\sqrt[3]{64}$ **b** $\sqrt[3]{8}$ **c** $\sqrt[3]{125}$ **d** $\sqrt[3]{27}$ **e** $\sqrt[3]{1}$

Reflect and reason

Miguel writes
$\sqrt[3]{1000}$ is 10 or -10.
Explain why he is incorrect.

Purposeful practice 3

Work out

1 $2^2 + 8$

2 $2^2 \times 8$

3 $8 - 2^2$

4 $8 \div 2^2$

5 $\sqrt{16} + 8$

6 $\sqrt{16} \times 8$

7 $8 - \sqrt{16}$

8 $8 \div \sqrt{16}$

9 $8 + \sqrt[3]{64}$

10 $8 \times \sqrt[3]{64}$

11 $\sqrt[3]{64} - 8$

12 $\sqrt[3]{64} \div 8$

Reflect and reason

Why do **Q1**, **Q5** and **Q9** (and also **Q2**, **Q6** and **Q10**) have the same answer?

Problem-solving practice

1 Sam is asked to work out $(-3)^2$.
She writes
$(-3)^2 = -9$
Is Sam correct? Explain your answer.

2 Copy and complete each calculation, giving two answers where possible.

a $\square^2 = 36$

b $\square^2 = 81$

c $\square^2 = 144$

d $\sqrt{\square} = 3$

e $\sqrt{\square} = 7$

f $\sqrt{\square} = 10$

3 Wayne has 200 square tiles.
He wants to make as large a solid square as possible using his tiles, by arranging them into an equal number of rows and columns.

a How many tiles are in each row?

b How many tiles are left over?

4 Zach works out $(-6)^3$.
He writes
$(-6)^3 = -216$
Is Zach correct? Explain your answer.

5 Copy and complete each calculation, giving two answers where possible.

a $\square^2 + (-6)^2 = 100$

b $\square^2 \times \sqrt{4} = 162$

c $\square^2 \div \sqrt{4} = 50$

d $\sqrt[3]{125} \times \square^3 = 5$

e $\sqrt[3]{8} \times \square^3 = -2$

f $(-10)^2 \div \square^2 = 4$

6 Which numbers below 100 are both a square and a cube number?

7 Here are six calculations.
Which calculations have the same answer?

A: $\sqrt{121} - \sqrt[3]{1000}$

B: $(-2)^2 - 1^3$

C: $3^2 - 2^3$

D: $\sqrt[3]{64} \div 2^2$

E: $\sqrt[3]{125} \times (-3)^2$

F: $3^3 \times \sqrt{4} \div \sqrt{81}$

8 Sunny has 200 centimetre cubes.
He uses his cubes to make the largest solid cube possible.

a What is the side length of this cube?

b How many centimetre cubes will Sunny have left over?

c How many more centimetre cubes would Sunny need to make the side length of the cube 1 cm longer?

9 Which number gives the same answer when square rooted and cube rooted?

Key points

- To work out $\sqrt{\text{addition or subtraction calculation}}$, first work out the calculation then square root, for example, $\sqrt{40 - 4} = \sqrt{36} = 6$ or -6.
- To work out $\dfrac{\text{calculation 1}}{\text{calculation 2}}$, work out (calculation 1) ÷ (calculation 2), for example,
  $\dfrac{12 + 20}{10 - 8} = (12 + 20) \div (10 - 8) = 32 \div 2 = 16$

△ Purposeful practice 1

1 Work out

a $(6 + 2)^2$ **b** $(6 - 2)^2$ **c** $(6 \times 2)^2$ **d** $(6 \div 2)^2$

e $6^2 + 2^2$ **f** $6^2 - 2^2$ **g** $6^2 \times 2^2$ **h** $6^2 \div 2^2$

2 Work out

a $(10 + 5)^2$ **b** $(10 - 5)^2$ **c** $(10 \times 5)^2$ **d** $(10 \div 5)^2$

e $10^2 + 5^2$ **f** $10^2 - 5^2$ **g** $10^2 \times 5^2$ **h** $10^2 \div 5^2$

Reflect and reason

Use your answers to **Q1** and **Q2** to help you copy and complete the missing operation $(+, -, \times, \div)$ in this statement:

$(\text{number} \,\square\, \text{number})^2 = \text{number}^2 \,\square\, \text{number}^2$

Give all the possible answers (there is more than one).

△ Purposeful practice 2

1 Work out

a i $\sqrt{25} \times \sqrt{4}$ **ii** $\sqrt{16} \times \sqrt{4}$ **iii** $\sqrt{64} \div \sqrt{4}$ **iv** $\sqrt{100} \div \sqrt{25}$

  b i $\sqrt{25 \times 4}$ **ii** $\sqrt{16 \times 4}$ **iii** $\sqrt{64 \div 4}$ **iv** $\sqrt{100 \div 25}$

2 Work out these. Where the answer is a decimal, give your answer to 2 decimal places.

a i $\sqrt{25} + \sqrt{4}$ **ii** $\sqrt{16} + \sqrt{4}$ **iii** $\sqrt{64} - \sqrt{4}$ **iv** $\sqrt{100} - \sqrt{25}$

  b i $\sqrt{25 + 4}$ **ii** $\sqrt{16 + 4}$ **iii** $\sqrt{64 - 4}$ **iv** $\sqrt{100 - 25}$

Reflect and reason

Use your answers to **Q1** and **Q2** to help you copy and complete the missing operation $(+, -, \times, \div)$ in this statement:

$\sqrt{\text{number}} \,\square\, \sqrt{\text{number}} = \sqrt{\text{number} \,\square\, \text{number}}$

There is more than one correct answer. Give all possible operations.

△ Purposeful practice 3

Work out

1 a $14 + 6$ **b** $\dfrac{14 + 6}{5}$ **c** $\dfrac{14 + 6}{15 - 10}$ **d** $\dfrac{14 + 2 \times 3}{15 - 10}$

2 a $2^3 + 1$ **b** $\dfrac{2^3 + 1}{3}$ **c** $\dfrac{2^3 + 1}{2 + 1}$ **d** $\dfrac{2^3 + 1}{2 - 1}$

3 a $7^2 - 3^2$ **b** $\dfrac{7^2 - 3^2}{\sqrt{25}}$ **c** $\dfrac{7^2 - 3^2}{\sqrt{25} \times \sqrt{4}}$ **d** $\dfrac{7^2 - 3^2}{\sqrt{25} \times 4}$

4 a $(2 + 6)^2$ **b** $\dfrac{(2 + 6)^2}{2^3}$ **c** $\dfrac{(2 + 6)^2}{2^3 + 8}$ **d** $\dfrac{(2 + 6)^2}{2^3 \times 4 + 8 \times 2^2}$

Reflect and reason

Ali works out $\dfrac{(2 + 3)^2}{\sqrt{9 + 16}}$ as

$$\dfrac{2^2 + 3}{\sqrt{9} + \sqrt{16}} = \dfrac{7}{3 + 4} = \dfrac{7}{7} = 1$$

What two mistakes has Ali made? What is the correct answer to the calculation?

⊠ Problem-solving practice

1 Here are six calculations. Which of the calculations have the same answer?

A: $(4 \times 5)^2$ B: 20^2 C: $2^2 \times 10^2$

D: $(2 + 10)^2$ E: $5^2 \times 4^2$ F: $4^2 + 5^2$

2 Which is the odd one out? Explain why.

$$\boxed{\sqrt{100} \times \sqrt{9}} \quad \boxed{\sqrt{100 \times 9}} \quad \boxed{\sqrt{9 + 100}} \quad \boxed{\sqrt{9 \times 100}}$$

3 Choose two numbers from 1 to 10 and write them down.

- Add your numbers together.
- Now square your answer and write it down.

a Does this give the same answer as squaring the two numbers you started with and then adding the square numbers together?

b Are there any numbers that would give a different answer to part **a**?

4 Copy and complete.

$$\dfrac{(1 + 7)^2}{\Box^3} = 1$$

5 Copy and complete this calculation, using only the numbers 1, 2 and 3.

$$\dfrac{8^2 + \Box^3}{\Box - \Box} = 36$$

6 Copy and complete this calculation, using only the operations $+$, $-$, $\times$ and $\div$.

$$\dfrac{\sqrt{81} \,\Box\, 3^3}{3^2 \,\Box\, \sqrt{4}} = 2$$

7 Steve is asked to work out $\dfrac{(25 - 19)^2}{2^2 + 6}$

Steve works out the answer in stages and writes

$$(25 - 19)^2 = 6^2 = 36$$

So $\dfrac{(25 - 19)^2}{2^2 + 6} = \dfrac{36}{2^2 + 6}$

$36 \div 2^2 + 6 = 15$ so $\dfrac{(25 - 19)^2}{2^2 + 6} = 15$

Is Steve correct? Explain why.

1.6 More powers, multiples and factors

Key points

- $2^4 = 2 \times 2 \times 2 \times 2$; 2^4 is '2 to the power 4'.
  The small number is the index or power and shows how many 2s to multiply together.
- The result of multiplying numbers or letters together is called their product. For example, the product of 3 and 10 is $3 \times 10 = 30$.
- Prime factors are factors that are prime numbers. The factors of 36 are 1, 2, 3, 4, 6, 9, 12, 18 and 36. The prime factors are 2 and 3.
- All positive integers can be written as a product of prime factors. This is called prime factor decomposition. The product is often written using index form (numbers with powers).
- You can use prime factor decomposition to find the highest common factor (HCF) or lowest common multiple (LCM) of two or more numbers.

△ Purposeful practice 1

1 Write each product using powers.

    a $4 \times 4 \times 4 \times 4 \times 4$ **b** $5 \times 5 \times 5 \times 5$ **c** $6 \times 6 \times 6 \times 7 \times 7$

    d $6 \times 6 \times 7 \times 7 \times 7$ **e** $3 \times 5 \times 5 \times 7$ **f** $2 \times 3 \times 5 \times 5 \times 2 \times 2$

2 Work out

    a 3^3 **b** 3^4 **c** 3^5 **d** 10^3 **e** 10^4

    f 10^5 **g** 1^3 **h** 1^9 **i** 1^{20} **j** 10^1

Reflect and reason

Jack writes the product $3 \times 3 \times 5 \times 5 \times 3$ as

$3^2 \times 5^2 \times 3$

Does Jack's answer give the same answer as the original product?

How can you further simplify Jack's answer?

△ Purposeful practice 2

1 Copy and complete each factor tree for prime factor decomposition in two different ways.

    a 35   **b** 70   **c** 350   **d** 700

    e 42   **f** 84   **g** 420   **h** 56

2 Write the numbers in **Q1** as products of prime factors.

3 Where possible, write the numbers in **Q1** as products of prime factors using index form.

Reflect and reason

Here is the start of Sally's factor tree for prime factor decomposition of the number 75.

What mistake has Sally made?

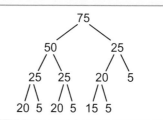

△ Purposeful practice 3

Use your answers to **Q2** in Purposeful practice 2 to work out

1 the highest common factor of

   a 84 and 700   **b** 420 and 700   **c** 56 and 84   **d** 84 and 420

2 the lowest common multiple of

   a 35 and 56   **b** 56 and 700   **c** 84 and 350   **d** 350 and 420

Reflect and reason

What is the same and what is different about using prime number decomposition for finding the HCF and the LCM of numbers?

⊠ Problem-solving practice

1 Lorna draws a factor tree for prime factor decomposition of the number 45.

Lorna has made two mistakes. What are they?

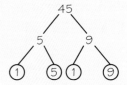

2 The HCF of two numbers is 45.
Is the statement 'one of the numbers could be 80' true or false?
Explain why.

3 **a** Write 60 as a product of its prime factors.

   b Write 12 as a product of its prime factors.

   c Does 60 divide by 12 exactly? Explain why using your answers to parts **a** and **b**.

   d Use prime factor decomposition to test whether $648 \div 36$ has a whole number answer.

4 Copy and complete

$72 = \square^3 \times \square^2$

5 The LCM of two numbers is 64.
Charlie says, 'Both numbers must have 2 as a factor.'
Is Charlie correct? Explain why.

6 Mrs Williams is organising the students in her school into teams.
She can group the students into teams of 25 or 45 without leaving any students out.
Work out the smallest possible number of students in the school.

7 Two bags of sweets are to be shared out equally into piles.
There are 60 red sweets in Bag A.
There are 84 yellow sweets in Bag B.
What is the greatest number of piles of sweets you can have?

8 Buses to Skipton leave a bus station every 20 minutes.
Buses to Burnley leave the same bus station every 24 minutes.
A bus to Skipton and a bus to Burnley both leave the bus station at the same time.
How long is it until another bus to Skipton and a bus to Burnley next leave the bus station at the same time?

9 Two numbers are replaced by ◇ and ☆.
Given that $◇ = 2^2 \times 3 \times 5$ and $☆ = 2 \times 3^2 \times 5$, what is the LCM of ◇ and ☆?

2 Area and volume

2.1 Area of a triangle

Key point

- Area of a triangle = $\frac{1}{2}$ × base length × perpendicular height

$$A = \frac{1}{2}bh$$

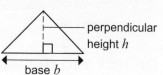
perpendicular height h

base b

△ Purposeful practice 1

Work out the area of each triangle.

1 a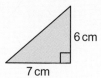
6 cm
7 cm

b
8 cm
10 cm
6 cm

c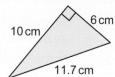
6 cm
10 cm
11.7 cm

2 a
5 cm
6 cm

b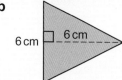
6 cm
6 cm

c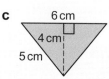
6 cm
4 cm
5 cm

3 a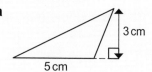
3 cm
5 cm

b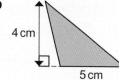
4 cm
5 cm

c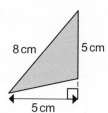
8 cm
5 cm
5 cm

Reflect and reason

Josie says the area of this triangle is 30 cm².
What mistake has she made?

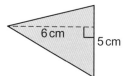
6 cm
5 cm

△ Purposeful practice 2

1 Follow the instructions below to work out the area of this triangle using three different methods.
State the way you find easiest.

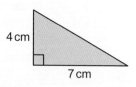
4 cm
7 cm

Method A	Method B	Method C
Halve the base and multiply by the height.	Halve the height and multiply by the base.	Multiply the base by the height. Then halve the result.
$\frac{1}{2} \times 7 \times \square =$	$\frac{1}{2} \times 4 \times \square =$	$7 \times \square = \square$
		$\square \times \frac{1}{2} =$

2 Repeat **Q1** for these triangles.

a
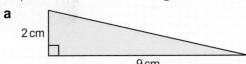
2 cm, 9 cm

b
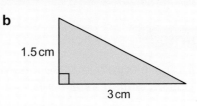
1.5 cm, 3 cm

Reflect and reason

Explain why all three methods in **Q1** work for finding the area.

Why is it useful to have three methods?

How do you decide which to use?

⊠ Problem-solving practice

1 Beth draws a right-angled triangle.
The sides that form the right angle have lengths 8 cm and 6.5 cm.
Work out the area of Beth's triangle.

2 Ruth, Sophie and Tristan each work out the area of the triangle.

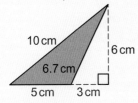
10 cm, 6 cm, 6.7 cm, 5 cm, 3 cm

Ruth writes

Area $= \frac{1}{2} \times 8 \times 6$
$= 24\,\text{cm}^2$

Sophie writes

Area $= \frac{1}{2} \times 5 \times 6$
$= 15\,\text{cm}^2$

Tristan writes

Area $= \frac{1}{2} \times 5 \times 6.7$
$= 16.75\,\text{cm}^2$

Who is correct? Explain why.

3 Which of these triangles have the same area? Explain why.

A 13 cm, 5 cm, 12 cm
B 9.9 cm, 7.3 cm, 7 cm, 9 cm
C 7.2 cm, 8.5 cm, 6 cm, 10 cm
D 18.4 cm, 4 cm, 15 cm

4 Sketch and label two different triangles with an area of 24 cm².

5 The area of this rectangle is three times the
area of the triangle.
Work out the height of the rectangle.

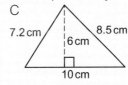
4 cm, 9 cm

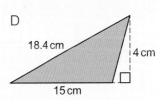
9 cm

6 Farah makes a kite from two identical triangles.
The height of the kite is 48 cm.
Calculate the area of the kite.

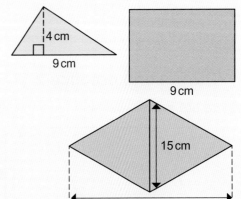
15 cm, 48 cm

Key points

- Area of parallelogram = base length × perpendicular height
  which can be written as $A = bh$

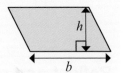

- Area of trapezium, $A = \frac{1}{2}(a + b)h$

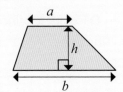

△ Purposeful practice 1

Calculate the area of each trapezium.

1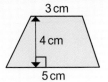
3 cm
4 cm
5 cm

2
3 cm
4 cm
7 cm

3
3 cm
4 cm
1 cm

4
3 cm
4 cm
2 cm

5
3 cm
4 cm
4 cm

6
2.5 cm
4 cm
3.5 cm

7
2.5 cm
2 cm
3.5 cm

8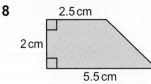
2.5 cm
2 cm
5.5 cm

9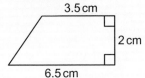
3.5 cm
2 cm
6.5 cm

Reflect and reason

Jonty works out the area of this trapezium.

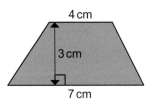
4 cm
3 cm
7 cm

Area = $\frac{1}{2} \times 4 + \underline{7 \times 3}$

= 2 + 21

= 23 cm²

Explain what Jonty has done wrong.

△ Purposeful practice 2

Here are some parallelograms and trapezia. Calculate the area of each quadrilateral.

1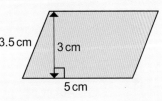
3.5 cm
3 cm
5 cm

2
3.5 cm
3 cm
5 cm

3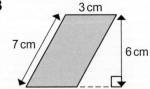
3 cm
7 cm
6 cm

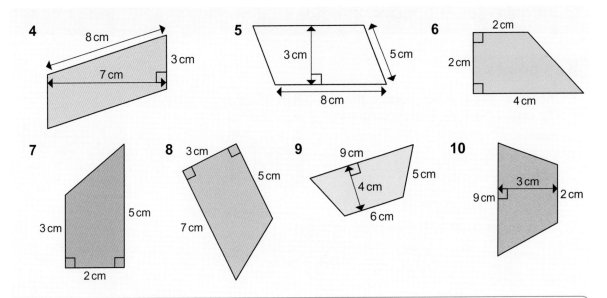

4 8 cm, 3 cm, 7 cm

5 3 cm, 5 cm, 8 cm

6 2 cm, 2 cm, 4 cm

7 3 cm, 5 cm, 2 cm

8 3 cm, 5 cm, 7 cm

9 9 cm, 5 cm, 4 cm, 6 cm

10 3 cm, 2 cm, 9 cm

Reflect and reason

When you use base and height in an area formula, does the base have to be horizontal and the height vertical? Use examples from this page to explain.

⊠ Problem-solving practice

1 Sketch and label two different parallelograms with an area of 36 cm².

2 Here is a trapezium drawn on a centimetre grid (grid not to scale).
The area of a parallelogram is the same as the area of the trapezium.
Write one possible set of measurements for the height and base of the parallelogram.

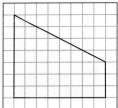

 3 This regular hexagon is made by joining two trapezia together.
Work out the area of the hexagon.

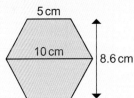

5 cm, 10 cm, 8.6 cm

 4 The trapezium shows a sketch of a swimming pool wall.
The wall is being tiled.
45 m² of tiles have been bought to tile the wall.
Will the tiles cover the wall? You must show your working.

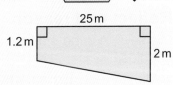

25 m, 1.2 m, 2 m

5 Kerry knows that these three trapezia all have the same height of 4 cm.

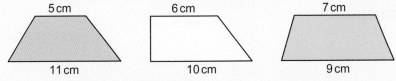

5 cm / 11 cm   6 cm / 10 cm   7 cm / 9 cm

Kerry says, 'Without calculating the area of each trapezium, I know that they all have the same area from the lengths of their parallel sides.'
Is Kerry correct? Explain why.

Key points

- The volume of a solid shape is the amount of 3D space it takes up.
  The units of volume are cubic units (e.g. mm^3, cm^3 or m^3).
- Volume of a cube, $V = l^3$

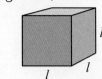

- Volume of a cuboid, $V = lwh$

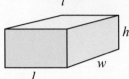

⚠ Purposeful practice 1

Calculate the volume of each 3D solid.

1
1 cm
1 cm
1 cm

2
1 cm
1 cm
2 cm

3
1 cm
2 cm
2 cm

4
2 cm
2 cm
2 cm

5
2 cm
2 cm
3 cm

6
2 cm
3 cm
3 cm

7
3 cm
3 cm
3 cm

8
4 cm
3 cm
3 cm

9
4 cm
4 cm
3 cm

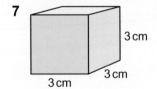
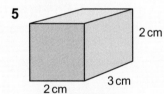
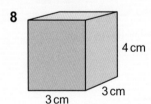
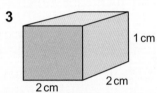
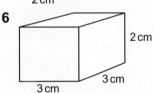
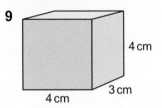

Reflect and reason

Mia says, 'A cube is a type of cuboid, so you can use the formula $V = lwh$ for cubes and cuboids.'

Is Mia correct? Explain why.

⚠ Purposeful practice 2

Calculate the volume of each 3D solid.

1
1 cm
1 cm
5 cm

2
2 cm
3 cm
5 cm

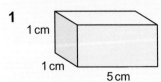
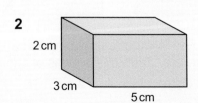

3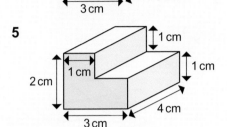

4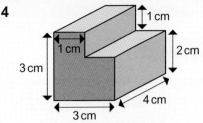

5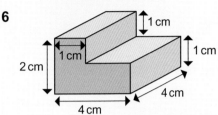

6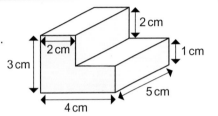

Reflect and reason

Here is Sophie's calculation for the volume of this solid.

$V = 3 \times 4 \times 5 = 60\,cm^3$

Explain what Sophie has done wrong.

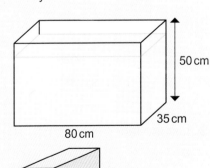

⊠ Problem-solving practice

1 Rory is working out the volume of a 2 cm cube.
He writes
Volume $= 2 \times 2 \times 2 = 6\,cm^2$
Is Rory correct? Explain why.

2 Sketch and label two different cuboids with volume $60\,cm^3$.

3 Will has a cube of side length 3 cm.
He says, 'The volume of any solid made with 8 of these cubes is $216\,cm^3$.'
Is Will correct?
You must show your working.

4 Grace puts wooden blocks into boxes. Each block is a 4 cm cube.
Each box is a cuboid, 12 cm by 20 cm by 20 cm. How many blocks will fit into a box?

5 Here is a fish tank.

  a What is the total volume of the fish tank?

Gavin pours water into the tank until the water is
5 cm from the top of the tank.

  b What is the volume of the water in the tank?

Gavin is buying gravel and sand for the fish tank.
He wants a 3 cm thick gravel and sand bed.

  c What volume of gravel and sand does
    Gavin need?

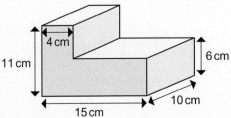

6 Ethan makes this solid from a cuboid
shaped block of wood.
Work out the volume of the cuboid cut away
from the block to make this shape.

Key points

- A 3D solid has faces, edges and vertices.
  Faces and edges can be flat or curved.

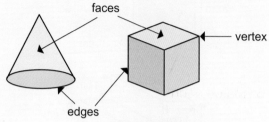

- A net is a 2D shape that folds to make a 3D solid.

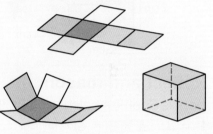

△ Purposeful practice

1 Match each 3D solid A–F to its net G–L.

A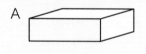

B

C

D

E

F

G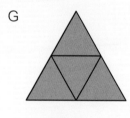

H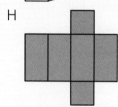

I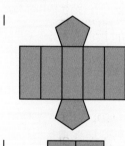

J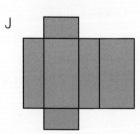

K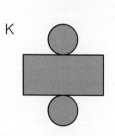

L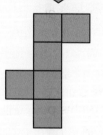

2 List the faces in each net. The first one has been started for you.

a

2 congruent rectangles,
☐ congruent right-angled _____
and 1 more rectangle

b

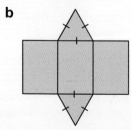

c 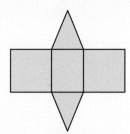   **d**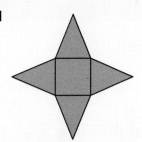

3 Match each 3D solid to one of the nets in **Q2**.

a    **b**   **c** 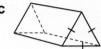   **d**

Reflect and reason

How can you use the shapes of faces of a 3D solid to help you identify its net?

⊠ Problem-solving practice

1 The diagram shows a cuboid.
Decide which of these nets, drawn on a centimetre square grid (grid not to scale), are possible nets for the cuboid.
Give reasons for each of your answers.

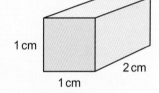

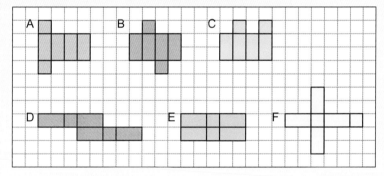

2 The diagram shows part of a net of a cube.

a Copy the diagram and add two squares to complete the net.

b Shade any two squares on your net such that opposite faces of the cube would be shaded when the cube is built.

3 Copy this net of a triangular prism.
The net is folded to make the prism.
One other point meets at P.
Mark this point on the net with the letter P.

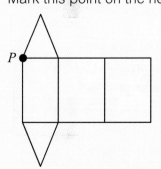

Key point

- The surface area of a 3D solid is the total area of all its faces.

⚠ Purposeful practice 1

For each 3D solid

   a write down the number of identical faces and a calculation for their area

   b calculate the total surface area

The first two have been started for you.

1 ☐ faces, area 4 cm × 4 cm   **2** ☐ faces, area 4 cm × 5 cm,   **3**

                                     ☐ faces, area 4 cm × 4 cm

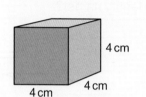
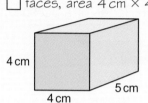
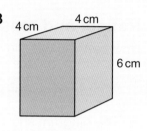

4
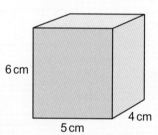

5
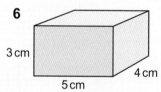

6

Reflect and reason

How does identifying identical faces help you calculate the surface area of a 3D solid?

⚠ Purposeful practice 2

1 Calculate the surface area of each cube.

  a   **b**   **c**

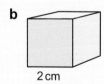
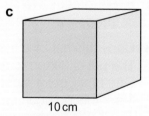

  1 cm   2 cm   10 cm

2 For a cube with each given surface area, work out

   i the area of one face   **ii** the length of one side

    a surface area = 54 cm²   **b** surface area = 150 cm²

    c surface area = 294 cm²   **d** surface area = 486 cm²

Reflect and reason

How have you used square numbers and square roots in these problems?

Problem-solving practice

1 Josh, Isabel and Freya are asked to work out the surface area of the cuboid.

Josh writes

Surface area = 10 × 7 × 6
= 420 cm²

Isabel writes

Surface area = 10 × 7 + 10 × 6 + 7 × 6
= 70 + 60 + 42 = 172 cm²

Freya writes

Surface area = 2 × 10 × 7 + 2 × 10 × 6 + 2 × 7 × 6
= 140 + 120 + 84 = 344 cm²

Who is correct? Explain why.

2 a For each calculation of surface area, write which cuboid A–D it matches.
One of the calculations does not match any of the cuboids.

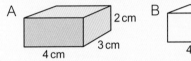
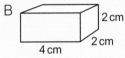
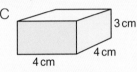
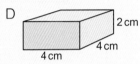

i 2 × 4 × 4 + 4 × 2 × 4   **ii** 2 × 3 × 2 + 2 × 4 × 3 + 2 × 4 × 2

iii 2 × 3 × 3 + 4 × 3 × 2   **iv** 2 × 2 × 2 + 4 × 2 × 4

v 2 × 4 × 4 + 4 × 3 × 4

b Sketch and label the cuboid for the calculation that didn't match one of the cuboids shown.

3 A cube has surface area of 96 cm².
Work out the side length of the cube.

4 Here are two open-topped boxes with the same volume. Which box has the smaller surface area? You must show your working.

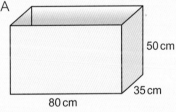
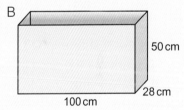

5 Five identical strips of wood are to be varnished. Each strip of wood is a cuboid measuring 3 cm by 450 cm by 20 cm. A can of varnish covers 100 000 cm². Will one can of varnish cover all five strips of wood? Explain why or why not.

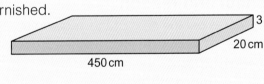

6 Jess has some cubes with a side length of 3 cm. She glues two of the cubes together. Jess says, 'The surface area of each cube is 54 cm². The surface area of the two cubes glued together is double this so is 108 cm².' Jess is incorrect. Explain why.

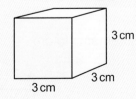
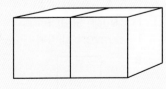

Key point

- 1 cm² = 100 mm²
  1 m² = 10 000 cm²

△ Purposeful practice 1

1 For each shape
  i convert all the measurements to mm
  ii work out the area in mm²

  a 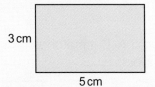 **b** 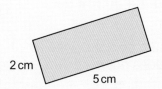 **c**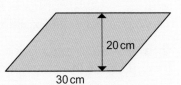

2 For each shape in **Q1**
  i work out the area in cm²
  ii convert the area to mm²

3 For each shape
  i convert all the measurements to cm
  ii work out the area in cm²

  a 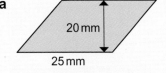 **b** 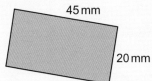 **c**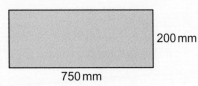

4 For each shape in **Q3**
  i work out the area in mm²
  ii convert the area to cm²

Reflect and reason

Rory works out the area of this rectangle
3 × 4 = 12 cm²
12 cm² = 120 mm²
What has Rory done wrong?

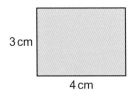

△ Purposeful practice 2

1 For each shape
  i convert all the measurements to cm   **ii** work out the area in cm²

  a   **b**   **c**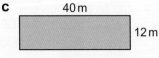

2 For each shape in **Q1**
   i work out the area in m²   **ii** convert the area to cm²

Reflect and reason

Explain how you would work out the area of each shape in the units given.

a

35 mm
20 mm
Area = ☐ cm²

b
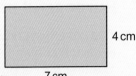
50 cm
120 cm
Area = ☐ mm²

⊠ Problem-solving practice

1 Isaac, Lexi and Sanjay are asked to work out the area of the rectangle in mm².

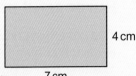
4 cm
7 cm

Isaac writes

Area = 4 × 7 = 28 cm²
1 cm = 10 mm
So 28 cm² = 280 cm²

Lexi writes

Area = 4 × 7 = 28 cm²
1 cm² = 10 mm × 10 mm
      = 100 mm²
So 28 cm² = 2800 mm²

Sanjay writes

Length = 70 mm, width = 40 mm
  Area = 70 mm × 40 mm
      = 2800 mm²

Who is correct? Explain why.

2 Show that the area of the parallelogram is the same as the area of the rectangle.

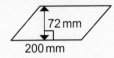
72 mm
200 mm

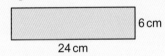
6 cm
24 cm

3 Work out the area of each shape, giving your answers in cm².

a
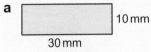
10 mm
30 mm

b
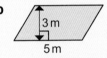
3 m
5 m

c

0.5 m
0.5 m

d
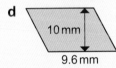
10 mm
9.6 mm

e
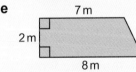
7 m
2 m
8 m

4 A parallelogram has a base of 48 cm and height of 120 cm.
Work out the area of the parallelogram, giving your answer in m².

5 Copy and complete the calculation for the area of a rectangle.
Area = 65 cm × ☐ cm = 0.91 m²

6 Sketch a rectangle that has an area of 72 cm².
Label your rectangle with its measurements given in mm.

7 Which of these shapes has the largest area? Explain why.

A
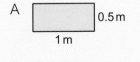
0.5 m
1 m

B
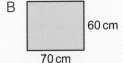
60 cm
70 cm

C
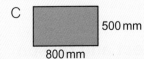
500 mm
800 mm

D
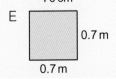
550 mm
850 mm

E
0.7 m
0.7 m

3 Statistics, graphs and charts

3.1 Pie charts

Key point

- A pie chart is a circle divided into slices called sectors. Each sector represents a set of data.

⚠ Purposeful practice 1

1 The pie chart shows the favourite subjects of 200 Year 7 students. For each subject, write the fraction and number of students. The first part is done for you.

   a maths

     fraction is $\frac{1}{2}$, number of students = $\frac{1}{2} \times 200 = 100$

   b science

   c English

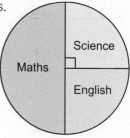

2 The pie chart shows the favourite subjects of 160 Year 8 students. For each subject, write the fraction and number of students.

3 The pie chart shows the favourite subjects of Year 9 students. 120 students chose maths.

   a How many students chose

     i English   **ii** PE   **iii** science?

   b Work out the total number of Year 9 students.

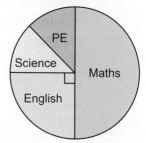

4 The pie chart shows the favourite subjects of Year 10 students. 45 students chose maths.

   a How many students chose

     i science   **ii** English?

   b Work out the total number of Year 10 students.

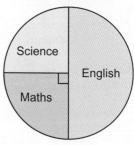

Reflect and reason

In **Q3** and **Q4**, do you need to work out the number of students who chose each subject to work out the total number of students?

1 The table shows the percentage of
   data and the angle to represent it
   in a pie chart. Find the missing values.

Percentage of data	Angle
100%	360°
50%	☐°
☐%	90°
10%	☐°
☐%	72°

2 Work out the angles for the pie
   chart for this data on hair colour.

Colour	Percentage	Angle
black	40%	
brown	20%	
blonde	25%	
red	10%	
grey	5%	

Reflect and reason
Did the table in **Q1** help you work out the angles in **Q2**? Explain.

⊠ **Problem-solving practice**

1 Year 8 students were asked for their favourite fruit.
   The pie chart shows the results.
   36 students chose apples.
   How many students are there in Year 8?

Favourite fruit

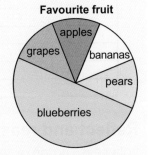

2 Year 7 students were asked for the guidance rating of the
   last film they watched.
   The pie chart shows the results.
   35 students watched a film with guidance rating 12A.
   How many students are there in Year 7?

Rating of films watched

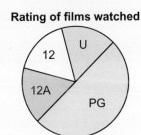

3 James is asked to draw a pie chart for the information given
   in the table.

Type of pet	Percentage
dog	40%
cat	30%
rabbit	20%
fish	10%

Types of pets

He draws the pie chart shown.
   a James's pie chart is incorrect. Explain why.
   b Draw a correct pie chart for the data.

Key point

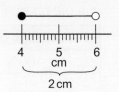

- The class $4 \leqslant l < 6$ includes all values of length l from $l = 4\,\text{cm}$ up to but not including $6\,\text{cm}$. The width of this class is $2\,\text{cm}$. $\leqslant$ means 'less than or equal to'.

 ⚠ **Purposeful practice 1**

Calculate the mean for each frequency table.

1

Number of lambs	Frequency
0	7
1	25
2	18

2

Number of passengers per car	Frequency
0	12
1	2
2	0
3	6

3

Test mark	Frequency
0	1
1	0
2	3
3	8
4	6
5	2

Reflect and reason

Lola says, 'If one of the values is zero, you can ignore that row in the table, because any number × 0 = 0.' Look at **Q2** and **Q3** and explain why Lola is wrong.

⚠ **Purposeful practice 2**

Here are the lengths of some leaves in cm.
3.8 cm, 2.1 cm, 12.6 cm, 4.2 cm, 13.9 cm, 5.7 cm, 10.4 cm,
7.5 cm, 11.8 cm, 9.0 cm, 6.1 cm, 8.6 cm, 5.2 cm, 3.1 cm
Copy and complete each table using these lengths. Make all your classes equal width.

1

Length	Tally	Frequency
$0 \leqslant l < 3$		
$3 \leqslant l < 6$		
$\square \leqslant l < \square$		
$\square \leqslant l < \square$		
$\square \leqslant l < 15$		

2

Length	Tally	Frequency
$2 \leqslant l < 5$		
$5 \leqslant l < \square$		
$\square \leqslant l < \square$		
$\square \leqslant l < \square$		

Reflect and reason

Find the smallest and largest values in the set of leaf lengths.

How can these help you work out the classes for **Q2**?

Do you always need to start the first class at zero?

1 Emma and Ben work out the mean for the data given in the table.

Goals scored	Frequency
0	3
1	7
2	8
3	0
4	2

Emma writes

Mean = (0 × 3 + 1 × 7 + 2 × 8 + 3 × 0 + 4 × 2) ÷ 5
= (7 + 16 + 8) ÷ 5 = 6.2

Ben writes

Mean = 0 × 3 + 1 × 7 + 2 × 8 + 3 × 0 + 4 × 2 ÷ 20
= 7 + 16 + 8 ÷ 20 = 23.4

Emma and Ben have each made a mistake.

a What mistake has Emma made?

b What mistake has Ben made?

c Find the correct mean.

2 A supermarket sells apples in bags.
The table shows the mass of some of the apples.

a Work out the mean mass of the apples.

b Another apple is weighed. It has a mass of 25 g.
Will the mean of the apples increase or decrease?
Explain why.

Mass of apple (g)	Frequency
24	5
25	0
26	3
27	7
28	5

3 A company makes the claim, 'On average there are 36 sweets in a bag.'
Harriet counts the number of sweets in some of their bags of sweets.
Her results are shown in the table.
Is the company's claim correct?

Number of sweets	Frequency
33	20
34	21
35	21
36	23
37	11
38	4

Key points

- In a set of n data values, the median is the $\frac{n+1}{2}$th one.

- A stem and leaf diagram shows numerical data split into a 'stem' and 'leaves'. The key shows you how to read the values.

⚠ Purposeful practice 1

For each data set, find

    a the number of pieces of data n **b** $\frac{n+1}{2}$ **c** the median

1 5, 7, 9

2 5, 7, 9, 10, 12

3 5, 7, 9, 10, 12, 15, 20

4 5, 7, 7, 9

5 5, 7, 9, 10

6 5, 7, 11, 12

7 5, 7, 9, 9, 12, 15

8 5, 7, 9, 10, 12, 15

9 5, 7, 9, 12, 12, 15

Reflect and reason

For the set of numbers 12, 15, 18, 20, 20, 21

Jo writes

$n = 6$, $\frac{n+1}{2} = \frac{7}{2} = 3.5$ so median = 3.5

Explain what Jo has done wrong.

⚠ Purposeful practice 2

1 Find the mode from each stem and leaf diagram.

a
```
1 | 0, 1, 4, 6
2 | 3, 3, 3, 3
3 | 2, 4, 4, 6
```
Key: 1 | 0 means 10

b
```
1 | 0, 1, 4, 6
2 | 3, 3, 3, 3
3 | 2, 4, 4, 6
```
Key: 1 | 0 means 1.0

c
```
1 | 01, 46
2 | 33, 33
3 | 24, 46
```
Key: 1 | 01 means £1.01

d
```
4 | 2, 3, 3, 5
5 | 4, 7, 7, 7
6 | 2, 3, 8
```
Key: 4 | 2 means 42

e
```
4 | 2, 3, 3, 5
5 | 4, 7, 7, 7
6 | 2, 3, 8
```
Key: 4 | 2 means 4.2

f
```
4 | 2, 3, 3, 3, 3, 5
5 | 4, 7, 7, 7
6 | 2, 3, 8
```
Key: 4 | 2 means 42

2 Find the range for each stem and leaf diagram in **Q1**.

3 Find the median for each stem and leaf diagram in **Q1**.

Reflect and reason

Three students find the mode, median and range of this data.

```
0 | 6, 8
1 | 3, 4, 7
2 | 1, 1, 5
3 | 2
```
Key: 1 | 3 means 1.3

	Kate	Leo	Jonah
Median	7	21	2.1
Mode	1	17	1.7
Range	2 − 6 = −4	26	2.6

Who is correct? Explain what the others have done wrong.

1 Joe has ten number cards.
He says, 'If I put the cards in order, starting with the smallest, the median will be the number on the fifth card.'
Is Joe correct? Explain why.

2 A number in this list is missing: 12, 13, ☐, 19, 21, 21
The median is 17.
What is the missing number?

3 A set of cards is numbered from 1 to 100.
Five of these cards are shown with one turned face down.

| 20 | 6 | 54 | 35 | ☐ |

   a What number could be on the face-down card if the median is 25?
   b What number could be on the face-down card if the median is 20?

4 Here is an incomplete list of marks gained by students in a Maths test, listed in order.
☐, 19, ☐, ☐, 24, 25, ☐, ☐, ☐, 30, 32, ☐, ☐, 37, 38, ☐, 45, 50, 52, ☐
The stem and leaf diagram shows the same data.

```
1 | 5 ☐
2 | 2 2 ☐ ☐ 7 7 7
3 | ☐ ☐ 2 5 ☐ ☐
4 | 1 ☐
5 | ☐ ☐ 5
```
Key: 1 | 5 means 15

   a Use the list of marks and stem and leaf diagram to fill in the gaps in both.
   b Work out the mode, median and range of the test marks.

5 The stem and leaf diagram shows the height of some plants in mm.
   a How many plants have been measured?
   b How many of the plants are over 60 mm?
   c What is the mode for all of these plants?
   d What is the median for all of these plants?
   e Work out the range for all of these plants.

```
3 | 4 9
4 | 2 3 7 9
5 | 4 6 6 6 7 7
6 | 1 1 2 5 7 8
7 | 3 5 8
```
Key: 3 | 4 means 34 mm

This stem and leaf diagram shows the heights of the same plants a week later.

A gardener claims that these plants grow at least 50 mm per week, on average, at this stage in their growth.

   f Is the gardener correct? Explain why.

```
 7 | 5
 8 | 7 9 9
 9 | 3 5 8
10 | 1 4 9
11 | 1 3 6 6 7
12 | 3 5 7 7 8 9
```
Key: 7 | 5 means 75 mm

Key point

- Statistics are values that represent a set of data. Mean, median, mode and range are statistics.

△ Purposeful practice 1

Here are five students' results in all maths tests over one year.

	Test 1	Test 2	Test 3	Test 4	Test 5	Test 6	Test 7	Test 8
Student A	6	6	6	6	6	6	6	6
Student B	4	5	5	4	5	5	5	5
Student C	5	6	6	5	5	7	7	5
Student D	4	8	5	7	7	5	6	8
Student E	1	5	10	4	8	3	1	4

1 Work out the range for each student.

2 Which student's marks were the most consistent (most similar) in all the tests?

3 Which student's marks were the least consistent in all the tests?

Reflect and reason

What does the range tell you about a set of data?

△ Purposeful practice 2

1 a Work out the mean test score for each student in Purposeful practice 1.

  b Which student had the highest mean score?

  c Which student had the lowest mean score?

2 a Draw a line graph to show the test scores for the student in **Q1b**.
  Use axes like the ones shown.

  b On the same axes, draw a line graph to show the test scores for the student in **Q1c**.

  c Does the student with the higher mean score always get a higher score than the other?

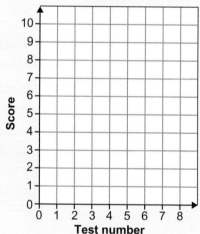

3 a Draw a line graph like those in **Q2** to show the test scores for students B and C from Purposeful practice 1.

  b Does the student with the higher mean score always get a higher score?

Reflect and reason

Two more students, F and G, took all the tests.
The mean for student F is 5.3 and the mean for student G is 7.1.
Jim says, 'This shows G always does better in the tests than F.'
Sally says, 'You can't tell who did better in each test from these statistics.'
Who is correct? Explain why.

⊠ Problem-solving practice

1 Andy and Rajiv recorded their results in weekly spelling tests over half a term.
   The table shows their results.

	Week 1	Week 2	Week 3	Week 4	Week 5	Week 6
Andy	6	10	12	5	10	11
Rajiv	7	8	6	9	10	8

   a Who spells more consistently? Explain why.
   b Who on average is the better speller? Explain why.

2 The Jones family are considering two different destinations for a holiday.
   The tables show the maximum temperature and amount of rainfall for these two
   destinations over a week.

Destination A	Day 1	Day 2	Day 3	Day 4	Day 5	Day 6	Day 7
Maximum temperature (°C)	29	30	32	30	30	30	29
Rainfall (mm)	0	0	2	5	0	0	0

Destination B	Day 1	Day 2	Day 3	Day 4	Day 5	Day 6	Day 7
Maximum temperature (°C)	33	32	33	34	33	32	34
Rainfall (mm)	86	0	102	10	96	50	125

   a Work out the mean temperature for each destination.
   b Work out the mean rainfall for each destination.
   c Work out the range in temperature for each destination.
   d Work out the range in rainfall for each destination.
   e Which destination do you think the Jones family should choose for their holiday
      if their main requirement is warm weather? Explain why using your answers to
      parts **a–d**.

3 The graph shows the average monthly temperatures for London (UK) and
   Christchurch (New Zealand) last year.

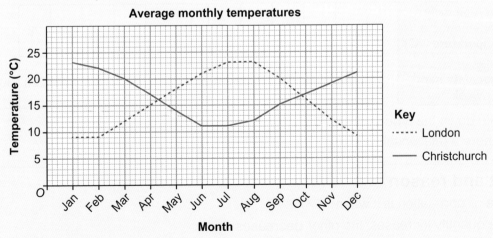

Average monthly temperatures

Key
······ London
——— Christchurch

Which of the two cities was warmer last year? Explain why.

Key points

- A scatter graph plots two sets of data on the same graph. The shape of the graph shows if there is a relationship or correlation between them.

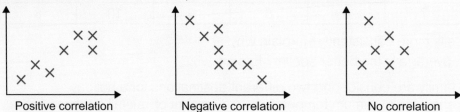

Positive correlation   Negative correlation   No correlation

- A line of best fit shows the relationship between two sets of data.

⚠ Purposeful practice 1

1 a Draw a scatter graph for this data from a camping and outdoors store.

Maximum temperature (°C)	1	2	3	4	5	6	7	9	10	11	12	13	15
Sales of gloves	46	50	42	48	42	38	40	30	34	24	38	20	14

  b Write down the type of correlation.

  c What happens to gloves sales as temperature increases?

2 a Draw a scatter graph for this data from a beach shop.

Maximum temperature (°C)	15	16	18	20	22	23	24	27	28
Sales of sunhats	12	24	22	28	30	38	44	42	48

  b Write down the type of correlation.

  c What happens to sunhat sales as temperature increases?

3 a Draw a scatter graph for this data from a convenience store.

Average daily maximum temperature (°C)	5	7	9	11	13	15	18	19	20	22	25	28	30
Sales of chocolate bars per week	300	240	200	380	160	400	340	180	100	240	200	220	300

  b Write down the type of correlation.

  c Is there a relationship between temperature and chocolate sales?

Reflect and reason

What type of correlation is it when

a as one quantity increases, the other decreases

b as one quantity increases, the other increases?

Purposeful practice 2

1 For each graph, which line is the correct line of best fit?

a 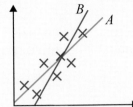 **b** 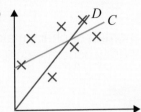 **c**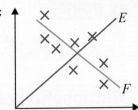

2 Draw lines of best fit on your graphs in **Q1** and **Q2** from Purposeful practice 1.

Reflect and reason

Does a line of best fit have to go through (0, 0)?

Does a line of best fit have to pass through some data points?

Use examples from this page to explain.

Problem-solving practice

1 Students sit two maths papers for a test.
The table shows the marks of 8 students.

Paper 1	27	32	40	53	55	61	68	73
Paper 2	30	37	50	55	61	62	70	72

   a Plot the data on a scatter graph.

   b Draw a line of best fit on your graph.

   c Describe the correlation between the marks for papers 1 and 2.

2 Describe the correlation for each data set.

   a

x	102	109	113	120	125	128	134	150
y	76	74	79	65	67	60	50	48

   b

x	350	360	375	425	440	480	510
y	27	82	65	74	33	59	48

   c

x	750	800	960	1100	1230	1420	1540	1680	1810
y	268	250	243	233	222	210	209	205	203

   d

x	5.1	5.3	5.4	5.7	6.0	6.3	6.3	6.4	6.6	7.1
y	12.3	11.9	12.1	12.5	12.5	12.6	13.0	12.9	13.9	14.0

3 For each relationship, describe the correlation you would expect, if any. Explain why.

   a House prices and number of students arriving late to school.

   b Amount spent on advertising a toy and sales of the toy.

   c The value of a car and its age.

   d The amount of rainfall and umbrella sales.

   e A student's height and their result in a maths exam.

   f A person's height and arm span.

3.6 Misleading graphs

Key point

- Before you read values from a graph or chart, make sure you read the title, axis labels and scales. You cannot draw accurate conclusions from an inaccurate graph.

⚠ Purposeful practice

1 Here are two identical pie charts.

A: Age groups in a judo club

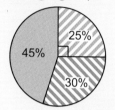

B: Colours of T-shirts sold

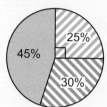

a Here are some questions on the pie charts. For each question, answer the question or say that more information is needed to do so.

Pie chart A questions

i How many age groups are there in the judo club?

ii How many judo club members are over 26?

iii What is the modal age group?

Pie chart B questions

iv Are the same number sold of each colour of T-shirt?

v What colours are the T-shirts?

vi How many more grey T-shirts are sold than blue T-shirts?

b Here is the key for each pie chart.

Key for pie chart A
▨ 7–16 ◩ 17–25 ☐ over 26

Key for pie chart B
▨ blue ◩ red ☐ grey

Look at the questions on the pie charts again. Answer the questions you now have enough information to answer.

c There are 80 people in the judo club and 800 T-shirts. Answer the rest of the questions on the pie charts that you have been unable to answer so far.

2 Here is a bar chart.

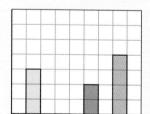

a Copy the bar chart.
Label the axes and give the bar chart a title so it represents this data.

Year	Number of holidays
2014	3
2015	0
2016	2
2017	4

b Copy the bar chart again.
Label the axes and give the bar chart a title so it represents this data.

Colour of car	Frequency
silver	15
purple	0
black	10
red	20

Reflect and reason

What information do you need to be able to interpret

a a pie chart

b a bar chart?

⊠ Problem-solving practice

1 The pie charts show the favourite weekend activities of Year 8 students at two different schools.

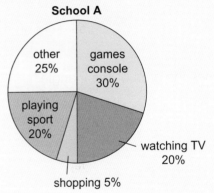
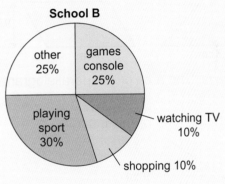

a What is the favourite activity for Year 8 students at school A?

b What is the favourite activity for Year 8 students at school B?

There are 120 Year 8 students at school A.

c How many students at school A prefer watching TV?

There are 200 Year 8 students at school B.

d How many students at school B prefer watching TV?

Tyler says, 'The sector for playing on games consoles in the pie chart for school A is bigger than the sector in the pie chart for school B. This means more students from school A prefer playing on games consoles than students from school B.'

e Is Tyler correct? Explain why.

2 The bar chart shows the number of students at a school with birthdays in the first half of the school year compared to the second half of the school year.

Kerry says, 'Around double the number of students have their birthdays in the first half of the school year.'

Is she correct? Explain why.

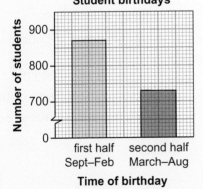

Mixed exercises A

1 Mrs Patterson wins £4311.
She shares the money equally between her 12 grandchildren.
Work out how much each grandchild receives.

2 Fay writes the number −7.
Suha writes the number −1.
Fay says, 'My number is −7 times Suha's number.'
Is she correct? Explain your answer.

3 Tony writes
$5^2 = (−5)^2$ and $5^3 = (−5)^3$
Is he correct? Explain your answer.

4 Here are a triangle and a parallelogram.

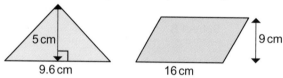

Mark says, 'The area of the parallelogram is six times the area of the triangle.'
Is he correct? Explain your answer.

5 Work out the area of this triangle.

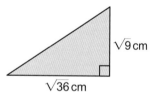

6 The table shows the average
temperature on each of six days
and the number of units of gas
used to heat a house on these days.

Average temperature (°C)	5	7	11	15	17
Units of gas used	15	12	6	2	0

  a Draw a scatter graph to show the information in the table.

  b Describe the relationship between the average temperature and the number of units of gas used.

  c Draw a line of best fit on your scatter graph.

7 Part of the net of a cuboid is drawn on centimetre squared paper.

  a Copy and complete the net of the cuboid.

  b Work out the volume of the cuboid.

  c Work out the surface area of the cuboid.

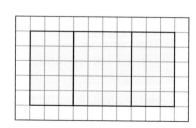

8 Here is a diagram of Pete's garden.
Pete wants to cover his garden with grass seed to make a lawn.
Grass seed is sold in boxes.
There is enough grass seed in each box to cover 50 m²
of garden.
Each box of grass seed costs £15.99.
Work out the smallest possible cost of grass seed if the whole garden is to be covered.

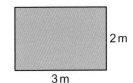

10 m   12 m

13 m

9 Here is a diagram of a wall in Jane's house.
Jane is going to cover this wall with square tiles.
The square tiles have sides of 20 cm.
Work out the number of tiles Jane needs.

2 m

3 m

10 There are 25 students trying out for a school football team.
12 of the students are in Year 7.
The heights, in cm, of the 12 Year 7 students are shown.

| 161 | 174 | 149 | 155 | 154 | 165 | 178 | 165 | 163 | 175 | 169 | 171 |

a Draw a stem and leaf diagram for the Year 7 students' heights.

There are 13 students in Year 8.
The heights, in cm, of the 13 Year 8 students are shown.

| 158 | 160 | 163 | 167 | 169 | 170 | 171 | 174 | 175 | 177 | 177 | 180 | 181 |

b Compare the heights of the Year 7 students with the heights of the Year 8 students.

11 A group of Year 8 students are asked to choose a new subject to study.
The table shows information about the subject they chose.

Subject	Number of students
Photography	56
Business studies	40
Tourism	24

a Draw an accurate pie chart to show this information.

A group of Year 9 students are also asked to choose a new subject to study.
This pie chart shows information about their choices.

Kieran says, 'The pie charts show that Business studies was chosen by more Year 9 students than Year 8 students.'

b Is he correct? Explain your answer.

Year 9 subject choices

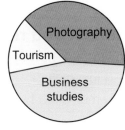

Photography

Tourism

Business studies

12 Jade and Ali set the alarms on their phones to sound at 7.15 am.
Both alarms sound together at 7.15 am.
Jade's alarm then sounds every 40 minutes.
Ali's alarm then sounds every 60 minutes.
At what time will both alarms next sound together?

13 The total surface area of a cube is 486 cm².
Work out the volume of the cube.

14 Luis is working out the mean from a frequency table.
One of the frequencies is missing from this table.
Luis finds out that the total number of books is 118.

Number of books per bag	Number of bags
5	11
6	☐
7	9

a Work out the missing frequency.

b Work out the mean.

4 Expressions and equations

4.1 Algebraic powers

Key points

- Index form means to write using a power or index. For example, 3×3 is written 3^2.
- In an algebraic expression, write numbers first and then letters in alphabetical order.

△ Purposeful practice 1

1 Write these products in index form.

a $x \times x$ **b** $x \times x \times x$ **c** $x \times x \times x \times x$

d $x \times x \times x \times x \times x$ **e** $t \times t \times t \times t \times t$ **f** $t \times t \times t$

g $t \times t \times t \times t$ **h** $t \times t$

2 Write each power as a product.

a m^4 **b** m^5 **c** y^3 **d** y^6 **e** y^2

3 Simplify these additions. The first one is done for you.

a $x + x = 2x$ **b** $x + x + x$ **c** $x + x + x + x$

d $x + x + x + x + x$ **e** $t + t + t + t + t$ **f** $t + t + t$

g $t + t + t + t$ **h** $t + t$

4 Write each term as an addition. The first one is done for you.

a $3y = y + y + y$ **b** $6y$ **c** $2y$ **d** $4m$ **e** $5m$

5 Write each term as a number × a letter. The first one is done for you.

a $3y = 3 \times y$ **b** $6y$ **c** $2y$ **d** $4m$ **e** $5m$

Reflect and reason

In algebra, how do you write

a 4 lots of a

b a multiplied by itself 4 times?

△ Purposeful practice 2

Write these products in index form. Some are started for you.

1 $2 \times 2 \times 3 = 2^\square \times 3$ **2** $2 \times 3 \times 3 = 2 \times 3^\square$ **3** $3 \times 3 \times 5$

4 $r \times r \times s = r^\square s$ **5** $r \times s \times s$ **6** $s \times s \times t$

7 $2 \times 2 \times 3 \times 3$ **8** $2 \times 2 \times 5 \times 5$ **9** $2 \times 2 \times 5 \times 5 \times 5$

10 $r \times r \times s \times s$ **11** $r \times r \times t \times t$ **12** $r \times r \times t \times t \times t$

13 $2 \times 3 \times 3 \times 3 \times 2 = 2^\square \times 3^\square$ **14** $3 \times 5 \times 5 \times 3$ **15** $5 \times 5 \times 2 \times 2 \times 2$

16 $r \times s \times s \times s \times r = r^\square s^\square$ **17** $s \times t \times t \times s$ **18** $t \times t \times r \times r \times r$

Reflect and reason

You can write $2 \times 2 \times 5 \times 2$ in index form as $2^3 \times 5$ or 5×2^3.
Is there more than one way to write $r \times r \times t \times r$ in index form?

1 Ian is asked to simplify $y \times y \times y$.
He writes
$y \times y \times y = 3y$
Is Ian correct? Explain why.

2 a The square has side length s.
Write a simplified expression for the perimeter of the square.

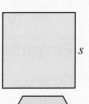

s

b The regular hexagon has side length h.
Write a simplified expression for the perimeter of the hexagon.

h

3 Which of these expressions is equivalent to x^5?
Explain why.

| $x + x + x + x + x$ | $x \times x \times x \times x \times x$ | $5x$ | 5^x |

4 Copy and complete this calculation, without using any powers.
$5 \times$ _____ $= 5^3 \times 7^4$

5 Jamal says, '$a \times a \times b \times b$ simplifies to ab^2 because a is squared and b is squared.'
Jamal is incorrect. Explain why.

6 Match each expression on the left with its simplified expression on the right.

A: $x \times x \times x \times x \times y \times y \times y$ G: x^5y^2

B: $x \times y \times x \times x \times x \times x \times x$ H: x^2y^5

C: $y \times y \times x \times y \times y \times y \times y$ I: x^4y^3

D: $x \times y \times x \times x \times x \times x \times y$ J: xy^6

E: $x \times x \times y \times y \times y \times y \times y$ K: x^3y^4

F: $x \times y \times x \times y \times y \times x \times y$ L: x^6y

7 Copy and complete
a $\square \times \square \times \square \times \square \times \square = a^2b^3$
b $\square \times \square \times \square \times \square \times \square = ab^4$

8 The term in each rectangle comes from multiplying the terms in the two circles that are linked to the rectangle.
Copy and complete the diagram.

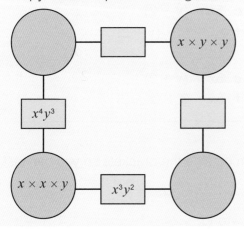

Key point

- To expand brackets, multiply each term inside the brackets by the term on the outside.

◁ Purposeful practice 1

1 Expand

   a $2(t + 3)$ **b** $-2(t + 3)$ **c** $2(t - 3)$ **d** $-2(t - 3)$

   e $2(3 + t)$ **f** $-2(3 + t)$ **g** $2(-3 + t)$ **h** $-2(-3 + t)$

   i $2(3 - t)$ **j** $-2(3 - t)$ **k** $2(-3 - t)$ **l** $-2(-3 - t)$

   m $2(5t + 3)$ **n** $-2(5t + 3)$ **o** $2(5t - 3)$ **p** $-2(5t - 3)$

   q $2t(5t + 3)$ **r** $-2t(5t + 3)$ **s** $2t(5t - 3)$ **t** $-2t(5t - 3)$

2 Expand and simplify

   a $5(x + 1) + 7$ **b** $5(x + 1) + 7x$ **c** $5(x - 1) + 7x$ **d** $5(x - 1) + 7$

   e $5(x - 1) - 7$ **f** $5(x - 1) - 7x$ **g** $10 - 5(x + 1)$ **h** $10 - 5(x - 1)$

   i $10x - 5(x + 1)$ **j** $10x - 5(x - 1)$ **k** $3 - 5(x + 1)$ **l** $3 - 5(x - 1)$

Reflect and reason

Sadie expands $-5(x - 3)$ to $-5x - 15$. Explain what she has done wrong.

When you multiply brackets by a negative number, what happens to the signs of both terms in the brackets?

◁ Purposeful practice 2

1 Simplify

   a $1 \times a$ **b** $-1 \times a$ **c** -1×4 **d** 1×-4

   e $-1 \times 4a$ **f** $4a \times -1$ **g** $-a \times -1$ **h** -1×-4

2 Copy and complete

   a $-(x + 2) = -1(x + 2) =$ **b** $-(x - 2) = -1(x - 2) =$

   c $-(2x + 1) = -1(2x + 1) =$ **d** $-(2x - 1) = -1(2x - 1) =$

3 Expand and simplify

   a $5 - (x + 2)$ **b** $5 - (x - 2)$ **c** $5x - (x - 2)$

   d $5x - (x + 2)$ **e** $5x + 1 - (x + 2)$ **f** $5x - 3 - (x + 2)$

4 Expand and simplify

   a $5 + (x + 2)$ **b** $5 + (x - 2)$ **c** $5x + (x + 2)$

   d $5x + (x - 2)$ **e** $5x + 1 + (x + 2)$ **f** $5x - 3 + (x - 2)$

Reflect and reason

Amit says, 'In these expressions, there isn't a term outside the brackets so you can just remove the brackets.'

$8 - (x + 5)$ $8 + (x + 5)$

Simplify the expressions and explain why Amit is wrong.

⊠ Problem-solving practice

1 Match each expression for the area of a rectangle with the correct rectangle.

a $12x + 6$ **b** $12x + 8$ **c** $12x + 10$ **d** $12x + 9$

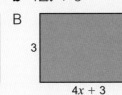

A — height 4, base $3x + 2$

B — height 3, base $4x + 3$

C — height 2, base $6x + 5$

D — height 6, base $2x + 1$

2 Copy and complete.

a $-3(a\,\square\,\square) = \square + 6$ **b** $-2(-5b\,\square\,\square) = \square + 14$

3 A question on expanding brackets gives the answer $4x - 8$.
What could the question have been?
Find as many different answers as you can.

4 In this algebra wheel, the opposite terms multiply to
give the expression in the centre.
Copy and complete the algebra wheel.

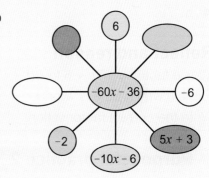

Centre: $-60x - 36$; spokes: 6, -6, $5x + 3$, $-10x - 6$, -2, and two blank.

5 An expression for the area of the rectangle is $15m^2 - 10m$.
The length of the rectangle is $3m - 2$.
What is the width of the rectangle?

width; base $3m - 2$

6 Match these expressions into equivalent pairs.

| $2(x - 3) + 7$ | $2(x - 4) + 7$ | $7 - (-2x + 3)$ | $7 + (-2x + 4)$ | $7 - (2x + 3)$ |

| $7 - (-2x - 3)$ | $-2x + 11$ | $2x + 10$ | $2x - 1$ | $2x + 4$ | $-2x + 4$ | $2x + 1$ |

7 Alice and Helen are asked to expand $4x - 5 - (x - 3)$.

Alice writes   Helen writes

$4x - 5 - (x - 3) = 4x - 5 - x + 3$ $4x - 5 - (x - 3) = 4x - 5 - x - 3$
$= 3x - 8$ $= 3x - 8$

Both Alice and Helen are incorrect.

a Explain what Alice has done wrong.

b Explain Helen's mistake.

c Write the correct answer.

Key points

- Expanding removes brackets from an expression.
  Factorising inserts brackets into an expression.

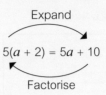

$$5(a + 2) = 5a + 10$$

Expand / Factorise

- To factorise an expression completely, write the HCF of its terms outside the brackets.

⚠ Purposeful practice 1

Factorise each expression. Check your answer by expanding the brackets.

1 a $3x + 9$ **b** $3x + 6$ **c** $3x + 3$

2 a $5a + 5$ **b** $5a + 10$ **c** $5a + 15$

3 a $4m - 12$ **b** $4m - 8$ **c** $4m - 4$

4 a $7y - 7$ **b** $7y - 14$ **c** $7y - 21$

Reflect and reason

Maisie factorises $6t - 6$ to $6(t - 0)$.

Explain why Maisie is wrong.

Write the correct factorisation.

⚠ Purposeful practice 2

Factorise each expression, and then check your answer by expanding.

1 a $6x + 9$ **b** $6x + 15$ **c** $6x + 21$

2 a $4a - 6$ **b** $4a - 10$ **c** $4a - 14$

3 a $15n + 10$ **b** $25n + 10$ **c** $35n + 10$

4 a $8h - 6$ **b** $8h - 10$ **c** $8h - 14$

5 a $8t + 12$ **b** $8t + 20$ **c** $8t + 28$

6 a $20y - 30$ **b** $20y - 50$ **c** $20y - 70$

7 a $a^2 + a$ **b** $a^2 - a$ **c** $2a^2 - a$
   d $2b^2 + b$ **e** $2b^2 + 3b$ **f** $3b^2 - 2b$
   g $5b^2 - 2b$ **h** $5b^2 - 3b$ **i** $5b^2 + 3b$

8 a $2c^2 + 6c$ **b** $2c^2 + 4c$ **c** $2c^2 + 2c$

9 a $3d^2 + 9d$ **b** $3d^2 + 6d$ **c** $3d^2 + 3d$

10 a $6e^2 + 9e$ **b** $6e^2 + 15e$ **c** $4f^2 - 6f$
   d $4f^2 + 14f$ **e** $8g - 12g^2$ **f** $8g - 20g^2$
   g $8g^2 - 20g$ **h** $20x^2 - 30x$ **i** $20x - 50x^2$

Reflect and reason

How can you tell that these expressions have not been factorised completely?

a $2(6x - 8)$ **b** $3(2p^2 - p)$ **c** $4(6m - 9m^2)$

1 Kris, Harry and Karen factorise $12x + 16$.

Kris writes   Harry writes   Karen writes

$12x + 16 = 4(8x + 12)$ $12x + 16 = 4(3x + 16)$ $12x + 16 = 4(3x + 4)$

  a Who is correct?

  b What mistake have the other students made?

2 Match these expressions into equivalent pairs.

$60t^2 - 25t$	$60t^2 - 14t$	$60t^2 - 50t$	$60t^2 - 48t$	$60t^2 - 16t$	$60t^2 - 42t$
$10t(6t - 5)$	$4t(15t - 4)$	$5t(12t - 5)$	$12t(5t - 4)$	$6t(10t - 7)$	$2t(30t - 7)$

3 Does $18a^2 - 27a$ factorise to $3(6a^2 + 9a)$? Explain why.

4 Copy and complete.

  a $10a - \square = \square(2a - 7)$ **b** $6b^2 + \square = 2b(\square + 7)$

5 Samar says, 'Factorising $20y - 28$ and factorising $35y^2 - 49y$ gives the same expression in the brackets.'

  Is Samar correct? Explain why.

6 Match each expression for the area of a rectangle with the correct rectangle.

  a $72y^2 + 60y$ **b** $72y^2 + 20y$ **c** $72y^2 + 56y$ **d** $72y^2 + 66y$

A
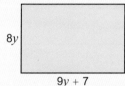
8y, 9y + 7

B
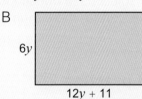
6y, 12y + 11

C
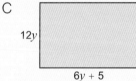
12y, 6y + 5

D
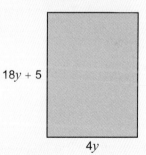
18y + 5, 4y

7 An expression for the area of a rectangle is $28h^2 - 35h$.

  a What is a possible width and length of the rectangle?

  b Write another possible width and length of the rectangle.

  c Which width and length of the rectangle is a complete factorisation of the area?

8 Isha is asked to factorise $4x^2 + 6x$ and $6x + 4x^2$.

  Isha says, '$4x^2 + 6x$ and $6x + 4x^2$ factorise to equivalent expressions.'

  a Is Isha correct? Explain.

  George is asked to factorise $12x^2 - 3x$ and $3x - 12x^2$.

  George says, '$12x^2 - 3x$ and $3x - 12x^2$ factorise to equivalent expressions.'

  b Is George correct? Explain.

Key points

- A function is a rule that changes one number into another. The function +3 adds 3 to a number.

  $2 \longrightarrow \boxed{+3} \longrightarrow 5$

  The inverse function is -3 because it reverses the effect of the function $+3$.

  $2 \longleftarrow \boxed{-3} \longleftarrow 5$

- An equation contains an unknown number (a letter) and an '=' sign. 'Solve an equation' means work out the value of the unknown number. The solution is the value of the unknown.

⚠ Purposeful practice 1

1 Solve

a $x + 7 = 7$ **b** $x + 7 = 6$ **c** $x + 7 = 5$ **d** $x + 7 = 0$

e $y - 7 = 0$ **f** $y - 7 = -1$ **g** $y - 7 = -2$ **h** $y - 7 = -4$

i $z + 30 = 25$ **j** $z - 30 = 25$ **k** $z - 30 = -25$ **l** $z - 5 = -8$

m $n - 5 = 0$ **n** $p - 5 = -30$

Reflect and reason

Hamza says, 'The solutions to questions in Purposeful practice 1 include $x = -7$, $x = 0$ and $x = 2$. How can x have more than one value?'

Explain why the value of x is not the same in every equation.

⚠ Purposeful practice 2

1 Solve each equation. The first has been started for you.

a $2x = 6$

b $2x = 18$ **c** $2x = 70$ **d** $2x = 0$

e $2x = 2$ **f** $3x = 15$ **g** $3x = 0$

h $3x = 6$ **i** $3x = 60$ **j** $4x = 60$

k $5x = 60$ **l** $6x = 60$ **m** $10x = 60$

n $12x = 60$ **o** $15x = 60$

2 Solve each equation. The first has been started for you.

a $\dfrac{n}{2} = 6$

b $\dfrac{n}{2} = 2$ **c** $\dfrac{n}{2} = 3$ **d** $\dfrac{n}{3} = 6$

e $\dfrac{n}{3} = 2$ **f** $\dfrac{n}{3} = 3$ **g** $\dfrac{n}{4} = 12$

h $\dfrac{n}{3} = 12$ **i** $\dfrac{n}{5} = 12$ **j** $\dfrac{n}{2} = 50$

k $\dfrac{n}{4} = 50$ **l** $\dfrac{n}{6} = 50$

3 Solve

a $4r = 12$ **b** $\dfrac{r}{4} = 12$ **c** $2t = 16$

d $\dfrac{t}{2} = 16$ **e** $\dfrac{m}{5} = 30$ **f** $5m = 30$

4 Solve

a $2y = -2$ **b** $2y = -4$ **c** $2y = -10$

d $-2y = 2$ **e** $-2y = 4$ **f** $-2y = 10$

g $-2y = -2$ **h** $-2y = -4$ **i** $-2y = -10$

Reflect and reason

Dale says, 'The solution to $\frac{x}{5} = 10$ is $x = 2$.'

Is he correct? Explain why. What mistake do you think he made?

◻ Problem-solving practice

1 Victor is asked to solve the equation $y - 6 = 10$. He draws the function machine shown and writes $y = 4$

Victor is incorrect. Explain why.

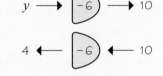

2 Here are eight equations. Match the equations into groups with the same solutions and give the solution for each group.

A: $6x = 42$ B: $\frac{x}{2} = 4$ C: $x + 23 = 30$ D: $7x = 63$

E: $8x = 64$ F: $x - 15 = -6$ G: $\frac{x}{3} = 3$ H: $27 + x = 35$

3 The perimeter of this rectangle is 36 cm.

  a Write an equation for the perimeter of the rectangle.

  b Solve your equation to find the value of n.

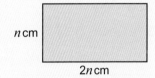

4 The area of this rectangle is 60 cm².

  a Write an equation for the area of the rectangle.

  b Solve your equation to find the value of x.

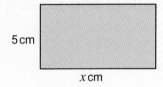

5 The perimeter of this square is 36 cm.

  a Write an equation for the perimeter of the square.

  b Solve your equation to find the value of s.

6 The angle sum of a full turn is 360°.

  a Write an equation for the angle sum of this diagram.

  b Solve your equation to find the value of a.

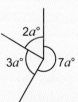

7 The volume of this cuboid is 60 cm³.

  a Write an equation for the volume of the cuboid.

  b Solve your equation to find the value of x.

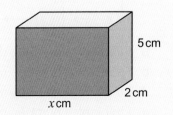

Key point

- You can use function machines to solve equations.
  For example, $2a + 1 = 9$

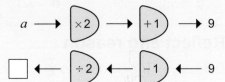

Purposeful practice 1

Solve these equations using function machines. The first two are started for you.

1 a $2x + 3 = 15$ **b** $2n - 3 = 15$

  c $2a - 5 = 15$ **d** $2b + 5 = 15$ **e** $2c - 15 = 5$ **f** $2d + 15 = 5$

2 a $3e + 5 = 11$ **b** $3f + 11 = 5$ **c** $3g - 5 = 7$
  d $3h - 7 = 5$ **e** $3k + 7 = 10$ **f** $3m + 10 = 7$

3 a $5n + 5 = 30$ **b** $5p - 5 = 30$ **c** $5q + 15 = 50$ **d** $5r - 15 = 50$
  e $5s + 50 = 100$ **f** $5t - 50 = 100$ **g** $5u + 100 = 50$ **h** $5v - 100 = 50$

Reflect and reason

Martin draws these function machines to solve
$2x + 6 = 14$.

Explain what Martin has done wrong.

$x \longrightarrow \boxed{+6} \longrightarrow \boxed{\times 2} \longrightarrow 14$

$1 \longleftarrow \boxed{-6} \longleftarrow \boxed{\div 2} \longleftarrow 14$

Purposeful practice 2

1 For each question part **a** to **e**,
  i draw a function machine for the situation described, using n for the number
  ii write an equation for the situation described
  iii solve the equation to work out the number, n
The first one is started for you.
  a I think of a number, double it and add 1. The answer is 17.

  i    **ii** $\boxed{}n + \boxed{} = 17$

  b I think of a number, double it and subtract 3. The answer is 17.
  c I think of a number, multiply it by 3 and add 5. The answer is 17.
  d I think of a number, multiply it by 3 and subtract 8. The answer is 16.
  e I think of a number, multiply it by 8 and subtract 3. The answer is 29.

2 Newspapers cost £x each and magazines cost £3 each.

    a Copy and complete the equation for the cost, in pounds, of 5 newspapers and 1 magazine.

    □x + □

    b 5 newspapers and 1 magazine cost £13.
    Copy and complete the equation for this information.

    □x + □ = 13

    c Solve your equation from part **b** to work out the cost of a newspaper.

Reflect and reason

How can drawing function machines help you write an equation?

⊠ Problem-solving practice

1 Amir is asked to solve the equation $2x - 8 = 22$.
Amir draws the function machines shown and writes

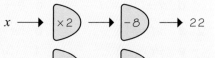

$x = 19$

Amir is incorrect. Explain why.

2 Priya thinks of a number. She multiplies her number by 6 and subtracts 5.
Her answer is 67.

    a Write an equation for Priya's number.   **b** What is Priya's number?

3 The diagram shows angles on a straight line.

    a Write an equation for the angles.

    b Solve the equation to find the value of a.

4 In the diagram, AC is a straight line and B is a point on the line.
$AB = 4x$ cm and $BC = 5$ cm.
$AC = 21$ cm

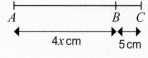

    a Write an equation for the length of the line.

    b Solve your equation to find the value of x.

5 The perimeter of this square is 28 cm.

    a Write an equation for the perimeter of the square.

    b Solve your equation to find the value of t.

$t + 3$ cm

6 **a** Solve

    i $5y - 26 = 24$ **ii** $5y - 10 = 40$ **iii** $5y - 5 = 45$ **iv** $5y - 20 = 30$

    v $5y - 2 = 48$ **vi** $5y - 44 = 6$ **vii** $5y - 13 = 37$ **viii** $5y - 38 = 12$

    b What do you notice about your answers? Explain why.

    c Is this also the case for the equation $10y - 30 = 20$? Explain why.

7 Here are six equations.

| $2x + 75 = 81$ | $2x + 1 = 81$ | $2x + 55 = 81$ | $2x - 11 = 81$ | $2x + 5 = 81$ | $2x - 75 = 81$ |

Which equation has   **a** the smallest value of x **b** the largest value of x?
Give the value of x in each case.

8 A plumber charges £P per hour plus a £25 callout fee.
The plumber works for 3 hours on a job and charges a total of £94.
Write and solve an equation to work out how much the plumber charges per hour.

Key point

- In an equation, the expressions on both sides of the equals sign have the same value. You can visualise them on balanced scales.

  The scales stay balanced if you apply the same operation to both sides. You can use this balancing method to solve equations.

◬ Purposeful practice 1

Solve these equations using the balancing method.

1 a $x + 7 = 12$ **b** $y - 7 = 12$ **c** $z - 12 = 7$
   d $a + 12 = 7$ **e** $b + 12 = -7$ **f** $c - 12 = -7$

2 a $5d = 15$ **b** $5e = -15$ **c** $-5f = -15$ **d** $-5g = 15$
   e $3h = 90$ **f** $-3i = 90$ **g** $3j = -90$ **h** $-3k = -90$

3 a $\dfrac{m}{2} = 10$ **b** $\dfrac{n}{2} = -10$ **c** $\dfrac{r}{2} = 5$
   d $\dfrac{s}{2} = -5$ **e** $\dfrac{t}{-2} = 5$ **f** $\dfrac{u}{-2} = -5$

4 a $2v + 3 = 19$ **b** $2w - 3 = 19$ **c** $5x - 3 = 27$
   d $5y + 3 = 28$ **e** $5z + 3 = -2$ **f** $5a - 3 = -8$

5 a $-2b + 3 = 11$ **b** $-2c + 5 = 11$ **c** $-2d + 7 = 11$
   d $-3e + 7 = 1$ **e** $-3f + 11 = 2$ **f** $-3g - 2 = 10$

Reflect and reason

Which is the correct method for solving $3x + 7 = 13$?

| $\div 3$ then $- 7$ | | $- 7$ then $\div 3$ |

Aurora says, 'To solve an equation, use the inverse functions in the reverse order.'
Use an equation from Purposeful practice 1 to show why Aurora is correct.

◬ Purposeful practice 2

1 The formula for the perimeter of a square is $P = 4s$.
   Work out the value of
   a P when $s = 7$ **b** s when $P = 12$

2 The formula for the area of a rectangle is $A = lw$.
   Work out the value of
   a A when $l = 7$ and $w = 5$ **b** l when $A = 20$ and $w = 5$
   c w when $A = 24$ and $l = 8$

3 The formula for the area of a parallelogram is $A = bh$.
   Work out the value of
   a A when $b = 8$ and $h = 6$ **b** b when $A = 8$ and $h = 2$
   c h when $A = 30$ and $b = 3$

4 The formula for the area of a triangle is $A = \frac{1}{2}bh$.
Work out the value of
a A when $b = 10$ and $h = 3$ **b** h when $A = 16$ and $b = 8$
c b when $A = 27$ and $h = 6$

5 The formula for the cost of hiring a car is $C = 20d + 100$, where C is the cost in £ and d is the number of days.
Work out
a the cost of hiring a car for 3 days
b the number of days for which the car hire cost is £200

> **Reflect and reason**
>
> When does using a formula to find a value involve solving an equation?

⊠ Problem-solving practice

1 The equation of a straight line is $y = 10x - 3$.
Work out
a y when $x = 5$ **b** x when $y = 117$

2 The formula for the area of a shape is $A = lw - 20$.
Work out the value of l when $A = 45$ and $w = 5$.

3 The formula for the perimeter of the rectangle is
$P = 2l + 2w$.

Work out the length, l, of the rectangle when $w = 7\,\text{cm}$ and
$P = 38\,\text{cm}$.

4 This rectangle has perimeter 24 cm.
a Work out the value of x.
b What is the length of the rectangle?

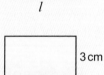

5 Work out the value of x.

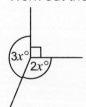

6 Sara is asked to solve $-2x + 9 = 17$.
She writes

$$-2x + 9 = 17$$
$$-9 \Big(\qquad \Big) -9$$
$$-2x = 8$$
$$+2 \Big(\qquad \Big) +2$$
$$x = 10$$

Sara is incorrect. What mistake has she made?

5 Real-life graphs

5.1 Conversion graphs

Key point

- A conversion graph converts values from one unit to another.

⚠ Purposeful practice 1

This conversion graph converts between kilograms (kg) and pounds (lb).

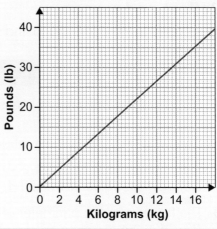

Kilogram/pound conversion graph

1 Use the graph to convert
   a 10 kg to pounds   b 33 lb to kilograms

2 Convert
   a 5 kg to pounds   b 1 kg to pounds
   c 66 lb to kg   d 1 lb to kilograms

Reflect and reason

When is it easier to use the graph to convert between pounds and kilograms? And when is it easier to do a calculation?

⚠ Purposeful practice 2

1 a Copy and complete this conversion table from centimetres to millimetres.

Centimetre	0	1	5
Millimetre			

   b Write
      i the highest cm value in your table
      ii the highest mm value in your table
   c On graph paper, draw
      i a horizontal axis for your cm values
      ii a vertical axis for your mm values
   d Plot the points from your table on the graph drawn in part **c**, and join them with a straight line.
      Give your graph a title.

2 Repeat **Q1** using this conversion table from miles to kilometres.

Miles	0	5	10
Kilometres		8	

Reflect and reason

How do you decide where to start and end your graph axes?
How do you choose the scale?

1 The graph converts between litres and pints.
Harrison has 2 litres of milk.
Tia has 3 pints of milk.
Who has the most milk? Explain why.

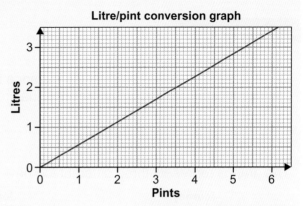

Litre/pint conversion graph

2 The graph converts between British pounds (£) and euros (€).
Carol buys a jacket on holiday costing 75 euros.
How much does the jacket cost in pounds?
You must show your working.

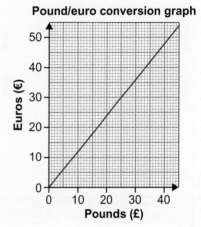

Pound/euro conversion graph

3 Amelia is asked to draw a conversion graph converting litres to gallons.
She is given the table to help her but she smudges some of the numbers in the table.
Amelia still has enough information to draw a conversion graph.
Use the table to draw a conversion graph.

Litres	●	4.55	●	●
Gallons	0	1	2	3

4 Zac is going on holiday to Australia.
He knows that £1 is worth 1.75 Australian dollars (AUD).
Draw a conversion graph up to £50 for Zac to use on holiday.

5 Alfie is on holiday in India.
She buys a book.
The cost of the book is 455 Indian rupees.
In England, the cost of the same book is £7.99.
The exchange rate is £1 = 90 Indian rupees.

  a Draw a conversion graph up to £10 for Alfie to use on holiday.

  b Use your graph to work out the difference in £ between the cost of the book in India and the cost of the book in England.

6 Helen has 32 litres of petrol in her car.
Dean has 8 gallons of petrol in his car.
One gallon is approximately 4.5 litres.
Who has more petrol in their car?
Draw and use a conversion graph to help you decide.

5.2 Distance–time graphs

Key point

- In a distance–time graph,
    the vertical axis represents the distance from the starting point
    the horizontal distance represents the time taken

⚠ Purposeful practice 1

The graphs represent three different journeys.

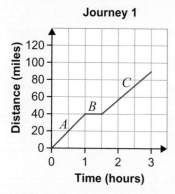
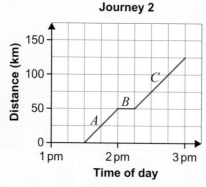
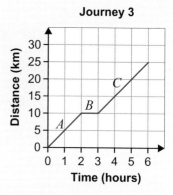

Copy and complete this table to describe each graph.

	Journey 1	Journey 2	Journey 3
A: Distance travelled			
A: Time spent travelling			
B: Time spent not moving			
C: Distance travelled			
C: Time spent travelling			
Total distance travelled			
Total time			

Reflect and reason

The graph lines for Journeys 2 and 3 are the same shape. Why are the journey descriptions not the same?

⚠ Purposeful practice 2

1 **a** Work out how far each car travels in one hour. Each car travels at a constant speed.

i Car A

40 km in $\frac{1}{2}$ hour

ii Car B

15 km in $\frac{1}{4}$ hour

iii Car C

180 km in 2 hours

b Which car in part **a** travels the fastest?

2 The graph shows a distance–time graph for car A.

  a Copy the graph. Add a title and axis labels.
     Draw lines on it to represent car B and car C.

  b Which car has the steepest line?

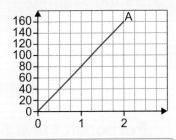

Reflect and reason

How can you tell from the graph in **Q2** that car B travels the slowest?

⊠ Problem-solving practice

1 Levi and Cameron cycle the same route from Leek to Derby and back again. The distance–time graph shows their journeys.

Levi starts cycling first, at 9 am. Cameron says, 'We both took 7 hours, so we travelled at the same speed for the whole of our journeys.'
Is Cameron correct? Explain why.

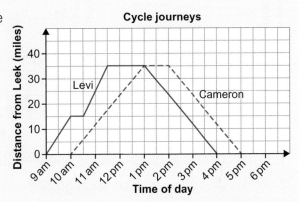

2 Milo walks 1.5 km to Kyle's house. Milo calls at the shop on his way. The distance–time graph represents Milo's journey.
Milo leaves the shop 8 minutes into his journey. He then walks at a steady speed for a further 13 minutes to reach Kyle's house.

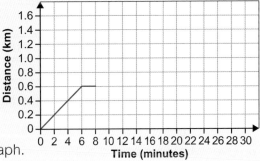

  a Copy and complete the distance–time graph.

  b For how long is Milo at the shop?

  c How far is the shop from Kyle's house?

3 Lily is competing in a triathlon that consists of a 1.5 km swim, 40 km bike ride and a 10 km run.
She completes her swim in 45 minutes, her cycle in $1\frac{1}{2}$ hours and her run in 1 hour.
Draw a distance–time graph to show her race.

4 Zoe has an electric scooter.
She travels 180 m in the first 100 seconds after leaving her house.
50 seconds later she has travelled another 180 m.
50 seconds later she has travelled another 210 m.
30 seconds later she has travelled another 160 m.

  a Draw a distance–time graph to represent Zoe's journey, assuming she travels at a constant speed during each section of her journey described.

  b Is Zoe getting faster or slower?
     Use your graph to explain your answer.

Key point

- The shape of a line graph shows whether a quantity is increasing or decreasing.

⚠ Purposeful practice 1

The graphs show information about the seaside town of Belleville.

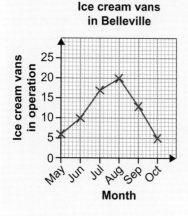
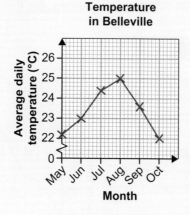
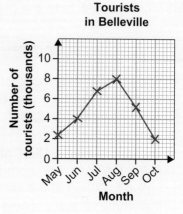

1 What does each graph tell you about August in Belleville?

2 What is the May value on each graph?

3 Copy and complete a table of values like this for each graph. Take the heading for the second row from the graph.

Month	May	Jun	Jul	Aug	Sep	Oct

4 What is the difference between the highest and lowest value on each graph?

5 Over what time period did the temperatures increase?

6 Over what time period did the number of tourists decrease?

Reflect and reason

Which two graphs can only represent whole number values? Explain why.

From which two graphs can you read the most accurate values? Explain why.

⚠ Purposeful practice 2

Draw a line graph for each set of data.
Choose a suitable scale for each axis.

1

Month	Jan	Feb	Mar	Apr	May	Jun
Rainfall (mm)	0	7	15	26	21	17

2

Month	Apr	May	Jun	Jul	Aug	Sep
Sales (£)	22 000	23 500	24 000	23 200	22 500	21 400

3

Year	2010	2012	2014	2016	2018
Maximum summer temperature (°C)	27.2	27.6	31.5	29.8	31.9

Reflect and reason

Which of your graphs has a vertical scale starting at 0?

Explain how you decided where to start the scale for each one.

⊠ Problem-solving practice

1 The line graph shows the maximum temperature recorded for each month during 2018 in London.

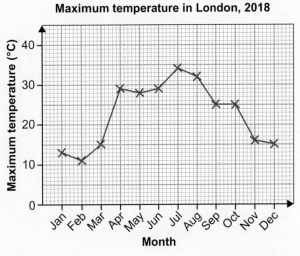

Maximum temperature in London, 2018

  a What is the biggest increase in temperature from one month to the next?

  b What is the biggest decrease in temperature from one month to the next?

  Jared says, 'The temperature increases every month from February to July and then decreases every month from July to December.'

  c Is Jared correct? Explain why.

2 The table and line graph show the cars sold by a car dealer each month for 6 months.

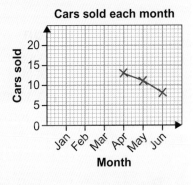

Cars sold each month

Month	Jan	Feb	Mar	Apr	May	Jun
Cars sold	12	9	19			

  a In which month did the car dealer sell the least amount of cars?

  b The car dealer sold 6 fewer cars in the months of July to December than he did from January to June during the same year.
  How many cars did the car dealer sell from July to December?

3 The table shows the average rainfall for Rosie's home town.
She draws the line graph to represent the data.
Write three things that are wrong with the graph.

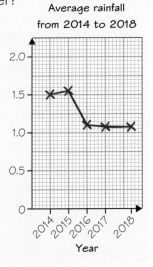

Average rainfall from 2014 to 2018

Year	2014	2015	2016	2017	2018
Average rainfall (m)	1.5	1.7	1.4	1.3	1.3

5.4 More line graphs

 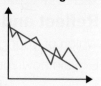
⚠ Purposeful practice 1

These scales show values in millions.

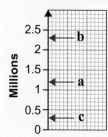 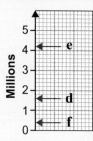 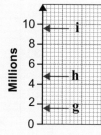 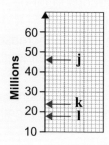

Write the value shown by each arrow
i in millions
ii as an ordinary number, written out in full
The first one is done for you.

a i 1.2 million   ii 1 200 000

Reflect and reason

Nadia says, 'To read this scale, I try counting up in steps of 0.1, 0.2, etc. until I find the ones that fit.'

Miles says, 'I see that 5 squares represent 1 000 000 so each small square represents $\frac{1\,000\,000}{5} = 200\,000$.'

Explain how **you** read a scale.

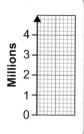

⚠ Purposeful practice 2

The table shows the emissions of sulfur dioxide and nitrogen oxides in the UK.

Year	1977	1987	1997	2007	2017
Sulfur dioxide (millions of tonnes)	5.1	3.9	1.7	0.6	0.2
Nitrogen oxides (millions of tonnes)	3.0	3.0	2.2	1.6	0.9

1 Draw a line graph for this data.

2 Describe the trends shown in the graph.

3 Estimate when the level of sulfur dioxide emissions first fell below the level of nitrogen oxides emissions.
   How does the graph show this?

4 Which emissions decreased most rapidly?
How does the graph show this?

Reflect and reason

On a graph like this, how can you show clearly which line represents which set of data?
Why is your answer to **Q3** only an estimate?

⊠ Problem-solving practice

1 The graph shows the population for Greater London during each census from 1951 to 2011.

Kelly says, 'The population for Greater London more than halved from 1951 to 1981 and then more than doubled again by 2011.'

Is Kelly correct? Explain why.

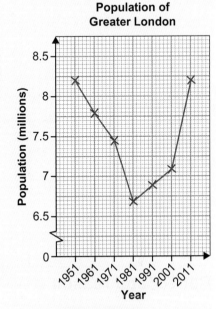

Population of Greater London

2 The graph shows the TV viewing figures for two programmes, A and B, over 10 weeks.

a Describe the trends of the viewing figures for both programmes.

b What is the greatest difference in viewing figures between the two programmes when

i programme A has the higher figures

ii programme B has the higher figures?

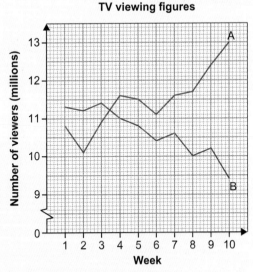

TV viewing figures

3 The table shows the monthly sales for two online shops over 6 months.

Month	Sep	Oct	Nov	Dec	Jan	Feb
Sales for shop A (£ millions)	0.8	1.5	1.3	1.5	1.8	2.8
Sales for shop B (£ millions)	1.3	1.2	1.5	1.4	1.7	2.1

a Draw a line graph for this data.

b Describe the trends shown in the graph.

c What is the greatest difference in sales between the two shops?

d What is the least difference in sales between the two shops?

5.5 Real-life graphs

⚠ Purposeful practice 1

The graph shows Lila's results in 5 maths tests.

1 Describe the trend shown by the graph.

2 The 'pass' mark is 50%.
How many tests did Lila pass?

3 Based on the graph, do you predict that
Lila will pass her next maths test? Explain.

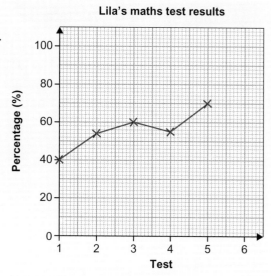

Lila's maths test results

Reflect and reason

In test 1, Lila got $\frac{8}{20}$ marks.

In test 3, Lila got $\frac{6}{10}$ marks.

Lila says, 'I got a higher mark in test 1. Why does it look lower on the graph?'
Explain why the graph is correct.

⚠ Purposeful practice 2

The graph shows information about people who
hold a driving licence in different age groups.

1 Give the percentage of people in the 26–70 age
group who held a driving licence in 1970.

2 Describe the trend for the 17–25 age group
between 1970 and 2010.

3 Describe the trend for the 26–70 age group
between 1970 and 2010.

Reflect and reason

Lucas says, 'The graph shows there were the same number of 17–25 driving licence
holders in 1992 and 1995.'

Thomas says, 'This may not be true.'

Explain what the graph actually shows and why Thomas is correct.

1 The table shows the cost for different numbers of ink cartridges from an online shop, including postage and packing.

Number of ink cartridges	1	2	5	10
Cost (£)	14.80	26.60	62.00	121.00

   a Draw a graph for this data.

   b The shop charges the same amount for postage and packaging regardless of how many ink cartridges Sophie buys.
      How much does postage and packaging cost?

2 The graph shows the percentage profit made by two companies.

   The director of company A says, 'Our percentage profit is decreasing overall as it fell from 2017 to 2018.'

   a Is the director correct? Explain why.

   The director of company B says, 'Our company made more money in 2016 than company A.'

   b The director may not be correct. Explain why.

   c From the graph, for which company do you predict the percentage profit is likely to remain about the same? Explain your answer.

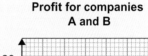
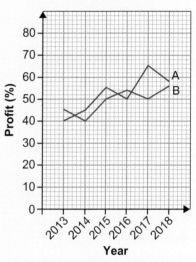

Profit for companies A and B

3 The graph shows the cost of getting work done by three different companies.
   Here are the charges of the three companies.
      Company X: Callout charge of £20 and £30 per hour.
      Company Y: Callout charge of £20 and £25 per hour.
      Company Z: Callout charge of £20, the first half hour is included in the callout charge and £32 per hour after the callout fee.

   a Match each line on the graph with the correct company.

   b What is the difference in cost between the cheapest and the most expensive company for a job taking 2 hours?

   c The company shown by line *A* is the most expensive company on the graph.
      Will this company always be the most expensive? Explain your answer.

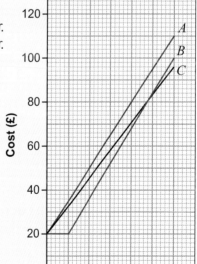

Cost of work

5.6 Curved graphs

△ Purposeful practice

1 Two samples of water are heated for 30 seconds.
The graphs show their temperatures.

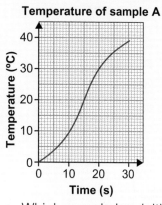

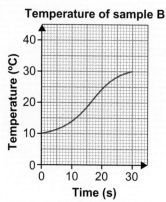

a Which sample has initial (starting) temperature

  i 0°C   ii 10°C?

b How many seconds does it take for sample A's temperature to increase by 20°C?

c How many seconds does it take for sample B's temperature to increase by 20°C?

d Which sample's temperature increases faster?

e Which graph curve is steeper?

2 The tables of values show the depth of water in two lakes between January and September.

Lake X

Month	Jan	Mar	May	Jul	Sep
Depth (m)	1.2	1.8	2.0	2.1	1.9

Lake Y

Month	Jan	Mar	May	Jul	Sep
Depth (m)	2.0	1.8	1.2	1.1	1.4

a Draw a graph for each lake.
  Plot the points from each table and join them with a smooth curve.

b Estimate the depth of lake X in June.

c In which two-month period does the depth of lake X increase the most?

d In which two-month period does the depth of lake Y decrease the most?

Reflect and reason

How can you tell from a curved graph
- whether a quantity is decreasing or increasing
- when it is increasing fastest?

⊠ Problem-solving practice

1 In a science experiment, calcium carbonate and sulfur
are heated together.
The graph shows the mass of each chemical as they
are heated.

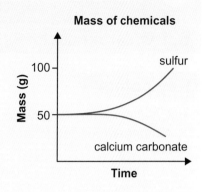

Mass of chemicals

  a Which chemical increases in mass as it is heated?
Explain how you know.

  b Which chemical decreases in mass as it is heated?
Explain how you know.

  c Seth says, 'The masses of calcium carbonate and
sulfur change at the same rate.'
Is Seth correct? Explain why.

2 Each of these containers is filled with water.
The water is flowing at a steady rate.
Match each container to the correct statement and correct graph.

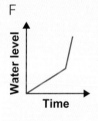 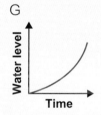 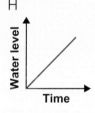 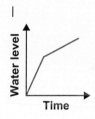 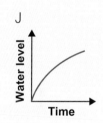

  A   The water level rises fast and then more slowly.
  B   The water level rises increasingly quickly.
  C   The water level rises increasingly slowly.
  D   The water level rises steadily.
  E   The water level rises slowly and then faster.

  F   G   H   I   J

3 Priya and Deana have a race over
400 m.
The graph shows information
about their race.

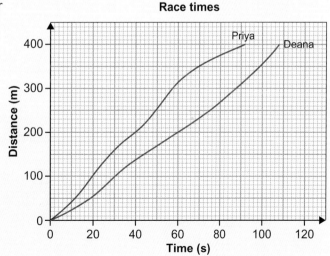

Race times

  a Who finishes the race first
and by how many seconds?
Explain how you know.

  b Did the person who finished
first run faster for the whole
race?
Explain how you know.

Unit 5 Curved graphs   **62**

6 Decimals and ratio

6.1 Ordering decimals and rounding

Key points

- A number rounded to two decimal places (2 d.p.) has two digits after the decimal point. A number rounded to three decimal places (3 d.p.) has three digits after the decimal point.
- For rounding to two decimal places, look at the thousandths (third decimal place): 0.005 and above round up, 0.004 and below round down.
  For rounding to three decimal places, look at the ten thousandths (fourth decimal place): 0.0005 and above round up, 0.0004 and below round down.
- You can round numbers to a certain number of significant figures (for example, 3 s.f.). The first significant figure is the one with the highest place value. It is the first non-zero digit in the number, counting from the left.

△ Purposeful practice 1

1 Round each number to
   i one decimal place   ii two decimal places   iii three decimal places
   a 905.6324   b 90.5632   c 9.0563   d 0.9056   e 0.0905

2 Round each number to   i one decimal place   ii one significant figure
   a 8.42   b 0.842   c 0.0842   d 0.008 42

3 Round each number to   i two decimal places   ii two significant figures
   a 40.0367   b 4.003 67   c 0.400 367   d 0.040 036 7

4 Each calculator display shows an amount of money. Round it to
   i two decimal places   ii three significant figures
   Give each answer in the form £□.□□

   a `2.493 7 16 25`   b `24.937 162 5`   c `249.37 1625`

   d `2493.7 16 25`   e `24937. 1625`   f `249371.625`

Reflect and reason

Is it more accurate to round money amounts to 2 d.p. or 3 s.f.? Explain why.

△ Purposeful practice 2

1 Copy and complete each calculation by writing '<' or '>' between each pair of numbers.
   a 0.4651 □ 0.6451   b 0.4651 □ 0.1465   c 0.4651 □ 0.4165
   d 0.4651 □ 0.4615   e 0.4651 □ 0.561   f 0.4651 □ 0.6
   g 0.4651 □ 0.461 59

2 Write each list of decimal numbers in descending order.

a 29.0061, 29.0601, 29.6, 29.6061

b 9.200 16, 9.020 16, 9.201 06, 9.216

c −3.724, −3.247, −3.4, −4.32

d 0.083, −0.803, 0.308, −0.83

Reflect and reason

Repeat **Q2**, but insert a new decimal into each list so that they are still in descending order.

⊠ Problem-solving practice

1 a A number rounded up to the nearest decimal place is 4.6.
Write one possible value this number could have.

b A number rounded down to the nearest decimal place is 4.6.
Write one possible value this number could have.

2 Which of these numbers round to the same value when rounded to 1 d.p. and 2 d.p.?

A 3.993   B 1.698   C 0.395   D 25.1964

3 Use the digits 1, 2, 3 and 4 to make two 4-digit numbers with three decimal places (use each digit only once in each number).
Write the numbers with '<' or '>' between them.

4 Is the statement 7.4 > 7.39 true? Explain why.

5 These numbers have been arranged in ascending order.
6.68, 6.79, 6.9, 6.805, 6.81
Which number is in the wrong place?

6 Cora says, '0.23 is smaller than 0.203 because 23 is smaller than 203.'
Cora is incorrect. Explain why.

7 Write three numbers that round to 6.74.

8 Copy and complete this number so it rounds to 4.23 to 2 d.p. and 4.230 to 3 d.p.
4.23☐☐

9 Copy and complete the list of ascending numbers.
12.5, 12.507, 12.7, 12.☐☐☐, 12.72

10 Arrange the digits 5, 6, 7, 8 and 9 into a number, in the format shown, that gives the same value when rounded to 1 d.p. as when rounded to 2 d.p. Use each digit exactly once.

a ☐☐.☐☐☐   **b** ☐.☐☐☐☐

11 Each number needs rounding to two significant figures.
Which numbers round up and which round down? Explain why.

a 0.1111...   **b** 0.2222...   **c** 0.3333...

d 0.4444...   **e** 0.5555...   **f** 0.6666...

g 0.7777...   **h** 0.8888...   **i** 0.9999...

12 Mrs Brown has £1000 to share between her three grandchildren. She uses a calculator to divide 1000 by 3. The calculator displays the answer as 333.333 333 3

a How much does each grandchild get?

b Can Mrs Brown give each grandchild an equal amount whilst giving away the entire £1000? Explain why or why not.

Key point

- You can use long multiplication to multiply larger numbers. When multiplying decimals, you can ignore decimal points and use long multiplication. Then adjust the answer by dividing by 10, 100, 1000, ...

△ Purposeful practice 1

1 Work out

a
```
    4 2 1
×       3
```

b
```
    4 2 1
×     2 3
```

c
```
    4 2 1
×   1 2 3
```

d
```
    3 6 2
×       4
```

e
```
    3 6 2
×     3 4
```

f
```
    3 6 2
×   3 3 4
```

g
```
    8 7 5
×       6
```

h
```
    8 7 5
×     1 6
```

i
```
    8 7 5
×   2 1 6
```

2 Work out

a 243 × 113
b 524 × 261
c 733 × 482
d 956 × 784

Reflect and reason

Caspar says, 'When working out 956 × 784, I multiply each digit in 956 by 4 then 8 then 7.'
Theo says, 'When working out 956 × 784, I multiply each digit in 956 by 4 then 80 then 700.'
Who is correct? How does your working for long multiplication help to explain this?

△ Purposeful practice 2

1 Work out

a 43 × 12
b 43 × 1.2
c 43 × 0.12
d 4.3 × 0.12
e 27 × 34
f 27 × 3.4
g 27 × 0.34
h 2.7 × 0.34

2 Work out

a 615 × 23
b 615 × 2.3
c 615 × 0.23
d 61.5 × 2.3
e 6.15 × 2.3
f 61.5 × 0.23

3 Work out

a 572 × 36
b 572 × 3.6
c 572 × 0.36
d 57.2 × 3.6
e 5.72 × 3.6
f 57.2 × 0.36

4 Work out

a 348 × 521
b 348 × 52.1
c 348 × 5.21
d 348 × 0.521
e 34.8 × 521
f 34.8 × 52.1
g 34.8 × 5.21
h 3.48 × 521

Reflect and reason

How could you use your answer to **Q2a** or **Q2b** to help you work out **Q2c**?
Peter works out **Q3e** and writes 5.72 × 3.6 = 205.92
How could he have used estimation to realise this answer is wrong?

Work out

1 6×1 **2** 6×0.1 **3** 6×0.01 **4** 49×1

5 49×0.1 **6** 49×0.01 **7** 173×1 **8** 173×0.1

9 173×0.01 **10** 52.8×1 **11** 52.8×0.1 **12** 52.8×0.01

Reflect and reason

How do multiplying by 0.1 and dividing by 10 relate to each other?

How do multiplying by 0.01 and dividing by 100 relate to each other?

What division calculation do you think is the same as multiplying by 0.0001?

⊠ **Problem-solving practice**

1 Liam is asked to work out 237×46. His calculation is shown.

     a Liam is incorrect. Explain why.

     b What is 237×46?

     c Use your answer to 237×46 to work out 23.7×4.6.

```
      2 3 7
    ×   4 6
    ─────────
    1 4 2 2
        2 4
  +   9 4 8
        1 2
    ─────────
    2 3 7 0
        1 1
```

2 Grace is asked to work out 3.29×5.6.
Her calculation is shown. Explain why she is incorrect.

```
        3 2 9
      ×   5 6
    ─────────
      1 9 7 4
          1 5
    + 1 6 4 5 0
          1 4
    ─────────
      1 8 4 2 4
          1 1
```

So $3.29 \times 5.6 = 184.24$

3 Does 23.5×8.7 give the same answer as 235×0.87? Explain why.

4 $847 \times 63 = 53361$. Use this fact to decide if each calculation is correct.

     a $84.7 \times 63 = 5336.1$ **b** $84.7 \times 6.3 = 53.361$ **c** $84.7 \times 6.3 = 533.61$

     d $8.47 \times 63 = 533.61$ **e** $8.47 \times 6.3 = 533.61$ **f** $847 \times 0.63 = 53.361$

5 Copy and complete each calculation using the fact $3.54 \times 0.6 = 2.124$.

     a $35.4 \times \square = 212.4$ **b** $\square \times 6 = 2.124$ **c** $354 \times 0.06 = \square$

     d $35.4 \times \square = 2.124$ **e** $\square \times 6 = 21.24$ **f** $\square \times 0.6 = 2124$

6 Look at the calculations on the cards.
Which calculations give the same answer as 5.97×6.41?

A: 59.7×641	B: 59.7×0.641	C: 597×0.641
D: 0.597×641	E: 597×0.0641	F: 0.597×64.1

7 Write three different calculations that give the same answer as 6.49×37.2.

8 This is the plan of a room.

     a Work out the area of the room.

Louise buys carpet costing £17.50 per square metre for the room.

     b How much does it cost to carpet the room?

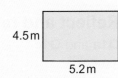

4.5 m

5.2 m

Key point

• When a calculation involves a number n divided by a decimal, first multiply both numbers by a power of 10 so that you are dividing by a whole number. For example

$$\times 10 \left(\begin{array}{c} 12 \div 0.2 \\ 120 \div 2 \end{array} \right) \times 10 \qquad \times 100 \left(\begin{array}{c} 12 \div 0.02 \\ 1200 \div 2 \end{array} \right) \times 100$$

△ Purposeful practice 1

1 Work out   **a** $32 \div 8$ **b** $3.2 \div 0.8$ **c** $32 \div 0.8$ **d** $3.2 \div 0.08$

2 Copy and complete

   a $18 \div \square = 6$ **b** $1.8 \div \square = 6$ **c** $18 \div \square = 60$ **d** $1.8 \div \square = 60$

Reflect and reason

Tyler works out $0.4 \div 0.2$. He writes $0.4 \div 0.2 = 0.8$

Describe two mistakes Tyler has made.

△ Purposeful practice 2

Work out

1	**a** 9×100	**b** 9×10	**c** 9×1	**d** 9×0.1	**e** 9×0.01
2	**a** $9 \div 100$	**b** $9 \div 10$	**c** $9 \div 1$	**d** $9 \div 0.1$	**e** $9 \div 0.01$
3	**a** 73×100	**b** 73×10	**c** 73×1	**d** 73×0.1	**e** 73×0.01
4	**a** $73 \div 100$	**b** $73 \div 10$	**c** $73 \div 1$	**d** $73 \div 0.1$	**e** $73 \div 0.01$
5	**a** 21.6×100	**b** 21.6×10	**c** 21.6×1	**d** 21.6×0.1	**e** 21.6×0.01
6	**a** $21.6 \div 100$	**b** $21.6 \div 10$	**c** $21.6 \div 1$	**d** $21.6 \div 0.1$	**e** $21.6 \div 0.01$

Reflect and reason

Copy and complete these statements.

$\div\ 100$ is the same as $\times \square$ $\div\ 10$ is the same as $\times \square$ $\div\ 1$ is the same as $\times \square$

△ Purposeful practice 3

1 Crista has £1043.62 in her bank account.

   a Sophie has $2\frac{1}{2}$ times as much as Crista. How much does Sophie have?

   b Andrew has £895.45 less than Sophie. How much does Andrew have?

   c Andrew's balance is 1.6 times as much as Isaac's. How much does Isaac have?

   d Jean has £399.50 more than Isaac. How much more does Jean have than Crista?

Reflect and reason

Q1a and **Q1c** include the word 'times'. Do you always multiply when a question includes 'times'?

⊠ Problem-solving practice

1 Match each pair of equivalent calculations.
   A: 4.7×1 B: 4.7×10 C: 4.7×100 D: 4.7×0.1 E: 4.7×0.01
   F: $4.7 \div 1$ G: $4.7 \div 10$ H: $4.7 \div 100$ I: $4.7 \div 0.1$ J: $4.7 \div 0.01$

2 Copy and complete
   a $5.2 \times \square = 520$ **b** $0.6 \times \square = 0.06$ **c** $\square \times 0.01 = 0.318$
   d $6.5 \div \square = 65$ **e** $73.2 \div \square = 0.732$ **f** $\square \div 100 = 0.23$

3 Olivia works out $0.6 \div 0.2$. She writes
   $0.6 \div 0.2 = 0.03$
   Olivia is incorrect. Explain why.

4 Umar spends £3.60 on sweets that cost £0.08 each.
   How many sweets has Umar bought?

5 The area of this triangle is $18.6 \, \text{cm}^2$.

   The area of the rectangle is three and a half times greater than the area of the triangle.
   Work out the area of the rectangle.

6 Angle a measures $80°$.
   Angle a is two and a half times the size of angle b.
   Work out the size of angle b.

7 The Smith family produces 0.97 tonnes of rubbish in a year.
   0.43 tonnes of this waste is incinerated. The rest is recycled.
   The Smith family recycles $1\frac{1}{2}$ times more rubbish than the Lee family.
   How much rubbish does the Lee family recycle?

8 A piece of red wool is 1.72 m longer than a piece of blue wool.
   The piece of blue wool is three and a half times the length of a piece of green wool.
   The piece of green wool is 4.83 m long.
   How long is the piece of red wool?

9 The probability of a spinner landing on red is 0.07.
   The probability of the spinner landing on yellow is 0.13.
   The probability of the spinner landing on blue is 0.25 more than on red.
   The probability of the spinner landing on green is $1\frac{1}{2}$ times that of landing on blue.
   Work out the probability that the spinner lands on green.

10 Sarah, Emily and Todd go shopping.
    Sarah spends £230.40.
    Sarah spends $4\frac{1}{2}$ times the amount Emily spends.
    Todd spends £75.80 more than Emily.
    How much does Todd spend?

Key points

- A ratio is a way of comparing two or more quantities.
- A ratio that includes decimal numbers can be multiplied to give an equivalent ratio with integers only. An example is shown:

  $\times 10 \left(\overset{0.5 : 1.2}{\underset{5 : 12}{}} \right) \times 10$

- A proportion compares a part and a whole. It may be written as a fraction (or decimal or percentage).
- You can compare ratios by writing them as unit ratios. In a unit ratio, one of the two numbers is 1, so it is written as 1 : ☐ or ☐ : 1.

⚠ Purposeful practice 1

1 Share £64 in each ratio.
   a 1 : 6 : 9   **b** 2 : 5 : 9   **c** 3 : 4 : 9   **d** 2 : 7 : 7   **e** 4 : 5 : 7

2 Share 160 m in each ratio.
   a 1 : 9 : 10   **b** 3 : 7 : 10   **c** 2 : 7 : 11   **d** 3 : 6 : 11   **e** 4 : 5 : 11

3 Share 750 g in each ratio.
   a 1 : 4 : 7 : 13   **b** 2 : 3 : 7 : 13   **c** 1 : 5 : 6 : 13   **d** 2 : 4 : 6 : 13   **e** 1 : 4 : 8 : 12

Reflect and reason

What did you notice about the total number of parts in the ratios in **Q1** parts **a–e** and **Q2** parts **a–e**?

⚠ Purposeful practice 2

For the counters in each of these board games, write
a the ratio of red : black : white counters   **b** the proportion of red counters
c the proportion of black counters   **d** the proportion of white counters

Give each ratio and proportion in its simplest form.

1 2 red, 4 black, 6 white   2 4 red, 6 black, 8 white   3 6 red, 8 black, 10 white

4 4 red, 6 black, 10 white   5 2 red, 4 black, 8 white   6 2 red, 4 black, 10 white

Reflect and reason

What do the fractions in **Q2**, **Q3** and **Q4** add to each time? Explain why.

⚠ Purposeful practice 3

1 Write each ratio as a whole number ratio in its simplest form.
   a 2 : 3.5   **b** 6 : 10.5   **c** 3 : 5.25   **d** 5 : 8.75
   e 1.6 : 2.4   **f** 10.8 : 14.4   **g** 1.1 : 1.21   **h** 1.2 : 6 : 0.3

2 Share £60 in the ratio
   a 0.5 : 1   **b** 0.5 : 1.5   **c** 1.25 : 6.25   **d** 1.5 : 2.25

3 Divide by the smallest number in the ratio to write these as unit ratios.
Give each answer to two decimal places.

   a 15 : 4   **b** 4 : 15   **c** 20 : 27   **d** 27 : 20
   e 48 : 35   **f** 35 : 48   **g** 101 : 3   **h** 3 : 101

Reflect and reason

To work out the answer to **Q1b**, Luke says, 'I multiplied both parts by 2, then simplified.'
Ahmed says, 'I multiplied both parts by 10 and then simplified.' Show that they both reach the same answer. Do both of their methods work for **Q1e**? Explain.

⊠ Problem-solving practice

1 Candice, Taylor and Salma are asked to simplify the ratio 3.6 : 6.

Candice writes   Taylor writes   Salma writes

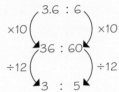

Who is correct? Explain why.

2 Copy and complete each statement.

   a 1.5 : ☐ simplifies to 3 : 7
   b ☐ : 2.4 simplifies to 1 : 6
   c 1.44 : ☐ : 2.56 simplifies to 9 : 7 : 16
   d ☐ : 9.6 : 12 simplifies to 3 : 4 : 5

3 Ryan, Jamie and Asha write the ratio 5 : 8 as a unit ratio.

Ryan writes   Jamie writes   Asha writes

Who is correct? Explain why.

4 Wei's recipe uses butter and flour in the ratio 1.05 : 1.4.
The ingredients he uses have a total mass of 280 g.
What mass of each ingredient does he use?

5 Alison and Finn share £300 in the ratio 2.86 : 1.54.
How much more money does Alison get than Finn?

6 A recipe uses flour, butter and sugar in the ratio 4 : 2.5 : 1.5.
Copy and complete the table to show the amount of each ingredient needed to make the quantity shown.

Recipe total	Flour	Butter	Sugar
800 g			
1 kg			
2.4 kg			

7 The table shows the quantities of fat, carbohydrates and 'other' in three ready meals.

   a Write the ratio of fat to carbohydrates to other for each meal.
   Simplify each ratio into a whole number ratio in its simplest form.

   b Write each ratio as a unit ratio, rounding your answers to 3 decimal places.

Meal	Fat	Carbohydrates	Other
A	24.6 g	46 g	279.4 g
B	13.6 g	60 g	326.4 g
C	27.5 g	90 g	332.5 g

7.1 Quadrilaterals

Key point

• The properties of a shape are facts about its sides, angles, diagonals and symmetry.

⚠ Purposeful practice 1

1 For each quadrilateral,
  i copy or trace the quadrilateral
  ii draw all its lines of symmetry
  iii use the lines of symmetry to identify equal angles and sides. Label equal angles with the same letter and equal sides with equal numbers of dashes.

  a rectangle   **b** rhombus   **c** kite   **d** isosceles trapezium

 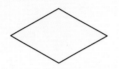  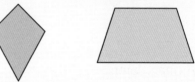

2 For each quadrilateral,
  i copy or trace the quadrilateral
  ii write down its order of rotational symmetry
  iii use the rotational symmetry to identify equal angles and sides. Label equal angles with the same letter and equal sides with the same number of dashes.

  a square   **b** parallelogram   **c** rhombus

Reflect and reason

How can you use symmetry of a shape to identify its equal sides and angles?

⚠ Purposeful practice 2

For each type of quadrilateral
a identify any equal angles
b work out the sizes of all angles labelled with letters

1 rhombus   2 parallelogram   3 isosceles trapezium

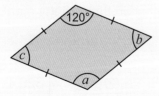 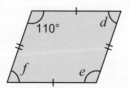 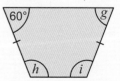

4 kite

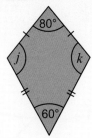

5 square

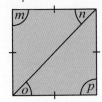

6 rhombus

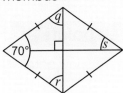

Reflect and reason

Farouk says, 'Opposite angles in a kite are equal, so $a = 40°$.'

Farouk is wrong. Explain the mistake he has made and work out the size of angle a.

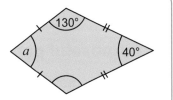

⊠ Problem-solving practice

1 Clare says, 'A quadrilateral has two lines of symmetry and rotational symmetry order 2.'
Name all the types of quadrilateral Clare could be describing.

2 A quadrilateral has four angles measuring 65°, 65°, 115° and 115°.
Name all the types of quadrilateral it could be.

3 The diagram shows a parallelogram.
Write the size of each angle.

4 Rachel says, 'The sides and angles of a rhombus are equal, so a, b and c are all 70°.'
Rachel is not correct. Explain why.

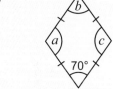

5 When shapes are congruent, they have the same shape and size.
The diagram shows two congruent rhombuses.
What is the size of each angle?

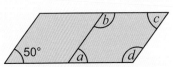

6 The diagram shows an isosceles trapezium.
Work out the size of each labelled angle.

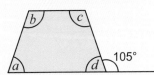

7 The diagram shows six congruent parallelograms.
Work out the size of angles a and b.

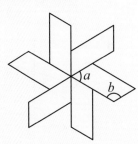

Key points

- We show parallel lines using arrows.

- When a line crosses two parallel lines it creates a 'Z' shape.
  Inside the Z shape are alternate angles.
  Alternate angles are equal.
  Alternate angles are on different (alternate) sides of the diagonal line.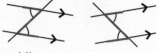

△ Purposeful practice

1 Which diagrams show a pair of alternate angles?

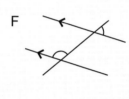

A   B   C

D   E   F

2 Identify the pair(s) of alternate angles in each diagram.
Write the sizes of the angles marked with letters.

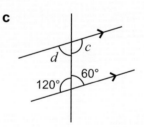

a   110°   70° a

b   100°   80° b

c d c 120°   60°

3 Work out the sizes of the angles marked with letters.
Give one of these reasons for each angle you find.

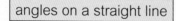

| alternate angles | angles on a straight line |

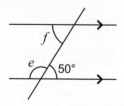

a f e 50°

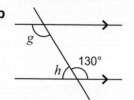

b g 130° h

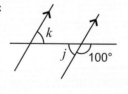

c k j 100°

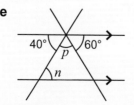

d   100° l m

e   40°   60° p n

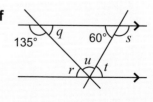

f   135° q 60° s r u t

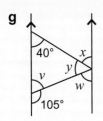

g

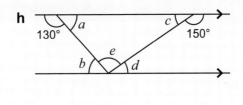

h

Reflect and reason

Poppy says, 'In this diagram, a and b are alternate angles because
- they are on opposite sides of the line
- one sits on a parallel line, the other 'hangs' from a parallel line.'

Use Poppy's definition to explain why x and y are **not** alternate angles.

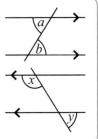

⊠ Problem-solving practice

1 Which pairs of angles are alternate? Explain why.

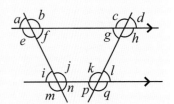

2 Work out the sizes of the angles marked with letters.
Give reasons for your answers.

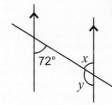

3 Noah works out angles a, b and c.
He writes

$a = 116°$ (angles on a straight line)
$b = 64°$ (alternate angles)
$c = 116°$ (angles on a straight line)

Noah has written some incorrect angles.
Which angles are wrong? Explain why.

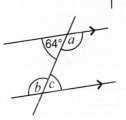

4 Jude is completing his homework on angles and parallel lines.
He works out that angle a is alternate to $55°$.
Sketch and label the diagram that Jude may have been given.

5 Work out the sizes of the angles marked with letters.
Give reasons for your answers.

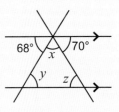

6 Chloe works out the size of angle a.
Chloe writes

$a = 130°$ because the angle $130°$ and angle a are alternate angles.
Is Chloe correct? Explain why.

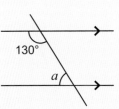

7.3 Angles in parallel lines

Key point

- When a line crosses two parallel lines it creates an 'F' shape.
  There are corresponding angles on an F shape.
  Corresponding angles are equal. Corresponding angles are on the
  same (corresponding) side of the diagonal line.

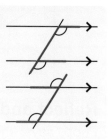

△ Purposeful practice

1 Which diagrams show a pair of corresponding angles?

A

B

C

D

E

F

2 Identify the pairs of corresponding angles in each diagram.
Write down the sizes of the angles marked with letters.

a

100°

a

b

b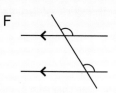

d

c

100°

c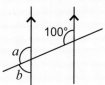

f

e 110°

d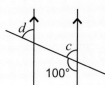

120°

h

i *g*

3 Work out the sizes of the angles marked with letters in each diagram.
Give one of these reasons for each angle you find.

corresponding angles		alternate angles
vertically opposite angles		angles on a straight line

a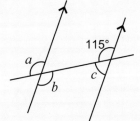

115°

a

b *c*

b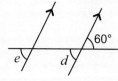

60°

e *d*

c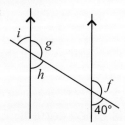

i

g

h

f

40°

75

d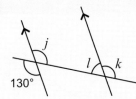

e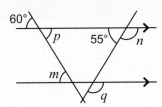

f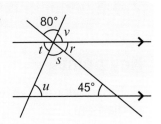

Reflect and reason

For **Q3e**, did you find angle n or angle p first? Work through the question again starting with a different angle to last time.

Is there always only one way to find the angles in parallel lines? Use more examples from this section to explain.

Problem-solving practice

1 Which pairs of angles are corresponding? Explain why.

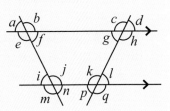

2 Sketch and label a diagram involving parallel lines with an angle of $60°$ and a corresponding angle x.

3 Work out the sizes of the angles marked with letters.
  Give reasons for your answers.

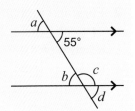

4 Here are some statements about the angles in the diagram.
  Decide whether each statement is true or false.
  Give reasons for your answers.
  a $a = f$ **b** $d = i$ **c** $b = j$
  d $a + b = g$ **e** $180 - m = n$ **f** $d = f$

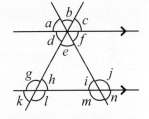

5 Work out the sizes of the angles marked with letters.
  Give reasons for your answers.

  a
  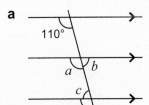

  b
  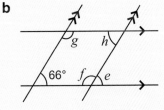

6 Work out the angles of this triangle.
  Give reasons for your answers.

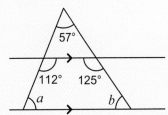

Key points

- The interior and exterior angles of a polygon are shown in the diagram.
- Sum of exterior angles of a polygon = 360°.
- Sum of interior angles of an n-sided polygon = $180°(n - 2)$.
- In an irregular polygon, sides are not all equal lengths and angles are not all equal.

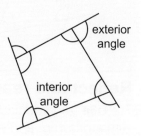

△ Purposeful practice 1

1 For each regular polygon,

   i calculate the sum of the interior angles using $180°(n - 2)$, where n is the number of sides

   ii work out the size of one interior angle

  iii work out the size of one exterior angle using 'angles on a straight line'

    a regular hexagon

    b regular octagon

    c regular decagon (10 sides)

    d regular 12-sided polygon

2 For each regular polygon in **Q1**

   i work out the size of one exterior angle using sum of exterior angles of a polygon = 360°

   ii work out the size of one interior angle using 'angles on a straight line'

  iii work out the sum of the interior angles using your answer to part **ii**

Reflect and reason

Which method did you find easier for finding

a the angle sum of a regular polygon

b the size of one interior angle of a regular polygon?

△ Purposeful practice 2

1 For each irregular polygon

   i calculate the sum of the interior angles

   ii work out the sizes of the angles marked with letters

a

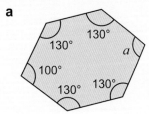

b

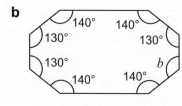

c

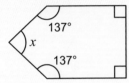

110°
110°
120°
100°
150°
150°
c

d

160° 140°
d
140°
140°
150°
140°
100° 170°

Reflect and reason

Why can't you use the method from **Q2** in Purposeful practice 1 to work out the size of an exterior angle of an irregular polygon?

⊠ Problem-solving practice

1 Work out the size of angle *x*.

137°
x
137°

2 Aaron works out the size of the interior angles of a regular octagon.
Aaron says, 'The interior angles of a regular octagon are 140° each.'
Explain how you know Aaron is incorrect.

3 Caitlin says, 'To work out each of the exterior angles in an irregular hexagon, divide 360 by 6.'
Is Caitlin correct? Explain why.

4 The spinner shown is a regular pentagon.
Work out the sizes of the angles marked with letters.

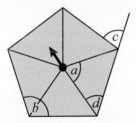

c
a
b *d*

5 Which regular polygon has interior angles that are double the size of its exterior angles?

6 The angle sum of a polygon is 900°.
How many sides does the polygon have?

7 The diagram shows a square and a regular pentagon.
Work out the size of angle *x*.

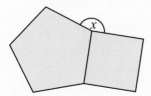

x

Key point

- You can solve a problem by writing an equation and solving it.

△ Purposeful practice 1

For each diagram

a write an equation

b solve your equation to find the value of the letter

c write down the sizes of all the angles, smallest first

1
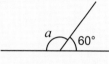

2
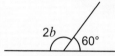

3
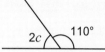

4

5
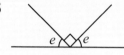

6
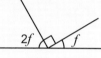

7
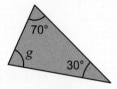

8
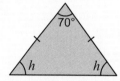

9
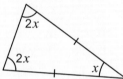

10
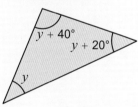

11
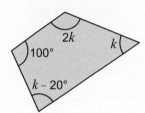

12
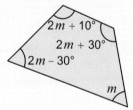

Reflect and reason

Danny is asked to work out the size of the angles in this triangle.

He writes

$4x - 20° = 180°$

$4x = 200°$

$x = 50°$

Has Danny solved the problem? Explain.

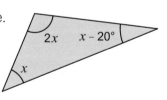

△ Purposeful practice 2

Write and solve an equation to work out the value of the letter in each diagram.

1

2

3
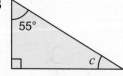

4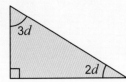

5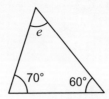

6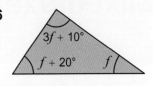

Reflect and reason

Did you need to write and solve an equation to find the angle in every question?

When would it be easier to work out the angle without an equation?

Problem-solving practice

1 Work out the missing angles in each diagram.

a

b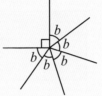

c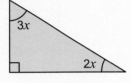

2 Work out the missing angles in each diagram.

a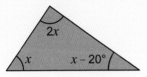

b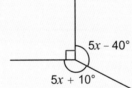

c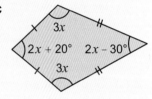

3 The size of the largest angle in a triangle is double the size of the smallest angle.
The other angle is 20° greater than the smallest angle.
Work out the size of each angle in the triangle.

4 In a parallelogram, the largest angle is 50° greater than the smallest angle.
What is the size of each angle in the parallelogram?

5 Work out the size of the angle labelled x.

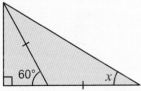

6 Work out the value of y.

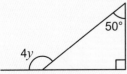

7 Work out the value of x and the value of y.

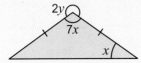

Mixed exercises B

Mixed problem-solving practice B

1 a Expand and simplify
$4x + 3(2x - 1)$

   b Solve
$4x + 3(2x - 1) = 57$

2 Older TVs have a screen width and height in the ratio 4 : 3.
Newer TVs have a screen width and height in the ratio 16 : 9.

   a Decide if each of these screens is old-style or new-style.

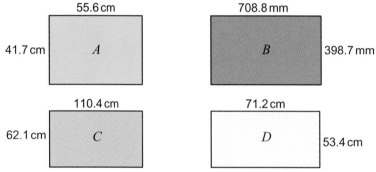

   b Work out the area of screen A.

3 a Show that an expression for the area of this
compound shape, in cm², is $14x + 23$.

   b The area of the shape is 79 cm².
Work out the value of x.

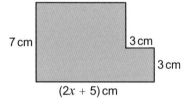

4 Work out the value of x and the value of y in the diagram.
You must show your working.

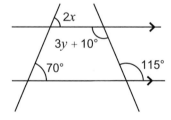

5 The cost £C of hiring a car for d days is given by the
equation $C = 45d + 40$.

   a One customer spends £310 on a hire car.

     i Write an equation for this hire involving d.

     ii Solve the equation to find the number of days
they hired the car for.

   b The graph shows the line $C = 45d + 40$.

     i Explain why point P gives the solution to the
equation in part **a**.

     ii Copy and complete this equation for Point Q:
$45d + 40 = \square$

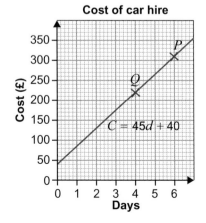

Cost of car hire

c Write and solve an equation to find the number of days the car is hired for when the car hire costs £445.

d What does the number 45 represent in the equation $C = 45d + 40$?

e What does the number 40 represent in the equation $C = 45d + 40$?

6 The diagram shows an irregular pentagon.
Work out the size of each angle in the pentagon.

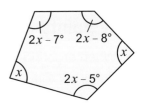

7 $ABCD$ is a quadrilateral.
The angles DAB, ABC, BCD and CDA are in the ratio $2 : 7 : 2 : 7$.
Work out the size of each angle.

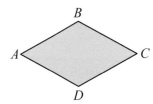

8 Two different shaped vases, A and B, are filled with water.
The graph shows the depth of water as each vase is filled.

a When is the depth of water in both vases the same?
Explain how you know.

b In which vase is the depth of water increasing faster in the first 10 seconds?
Explain how you know.

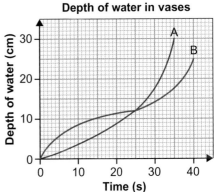

Depth of water in vases

9 Annabel and Kris each go on holiday.
Annabel goes to France and changes some pounds into euros.
Kris goes to Australia and changes some pounds into Australian dollars.
The graphs show the conversions for their money.

Conversion between euros and pounds

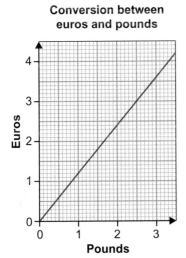

Conversion between Australian dollars and pounds

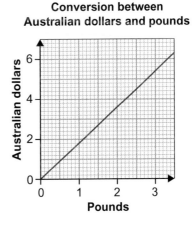

Annabel and Kris each have a meal out.
Annabel's meal costs 18 euros. Kris's meal costs 25 Australian dollars.
Who pays more for their meal? Explain why.

8 Calculating with fractions

8.1 Ordering fractions

Key points

- When ordering fractions, it can be useful to compare them to $\frac{1}{2}$.
- Fractions with the same denominator can be described as having a common denominator.
- When ordering fractions, it can be useful to compare their equivalent fractions, all written with a common denominator.

⚠ Purposeful practice 1

1. Copy each heading, then write each fraction in the box under one of the headings.

   'More than $\frac{1}{2}$'   'Equal to $\frac{1}{2}$'   'Less than $\frac{1}{2}$'

   | $\frac{1}{3}$ | $\frac{2}{3}$ | $\frac{1}{4}$ | $\frac{2}{4}$ | $\frac{3}{4}$ | $\frac{1}{5}$ | $\frac{2}{5}$ | $\frac{3}{5}$ | $\frac{4}{5}$ | $\frac{1}{6}$ | $\frac{2}{6}$ | $\frac{3}{6}$ | $\frac{4}{6}$ | $\frac{5}{6}$ |

2. Which of these lists of fractions are written in ascending order?

   A: $\frac{1}{3}, \frac{3}{6}, \frac{3}{5}$ B: $\frac{1}{4}, \frac{1}{2}, \frac{4}{5}$ C: $\frac{3}{5}, \frac{2}{4}, \frac{1}{6}$ D: $\frac{1}{5}, \frac{1}{2}, \frac{3}{4}$

3. Rewrite each list of fractions in descending order.

   a $\frac{3}{8}, \frac{1}{2}, \frac{3}{4}$ b $\frac{4}{8}, \frac{1}{4}, \frac{3}{4}$ c $\frac{5}{8}, \frac{1}{4}, \frac{1}{2}$

   d $\frac{2}{5}, \frac{1}{2}, \frac{3}{4}$ e $\frac{3}{10}, \frac{1}{2}, \frac{3}{5}$ f $\frac{5}{10}, \frac{2}{5}, \frac{5}{8}$

   g $\frac{6}{12}, \frac{8}{12}, \frac{2}{5}$ h $\frac{1}{5}, \frac{5}{6}, \frac{6}{12}$ i $\frac{3}{6}, \frac{1}{3}, \frac{7}{12}$

Reflect and reason

Look carefully at the fractions you listed under the different headings in **Q1**. What do you notice about the denominator compared to the numerator in the fractions in each list?

Why isn't it possible to write the fractions $\frac{3}{6}, \frac{10}{20}, \frac{6}{12}$ in descending order?

⚠ Purposeful practice 2

1. Write each list of fractions in ascending order. Find a lowest common denominator first, where necessary.

   a $\frac{3}{5}, \frac{1}{2}, \frac{4}{5}$ b $\frac{3}{5}, \frac{7}{10}, \frac{1}{2}$ c $\frac{1}{2}, \frac{7}{10}, \frac{13}{20}$

   d $\frac{7}{10}, \frac{2}{3}, \frac{1}{2}$ e $\frac{2}{3}, \frac{1}{2}, \frac{11}{18}$ f $\frac{3}{5}, \frac{17}{30}, \frac{1}{2}$

   g $\frac{13}{15}, \frac{23}{30}, \frac{1}{2}$ h $\frac{11}{15}, \frac{1}{2}, \frac{3}{5}$ i $\frac{1}{2}, \frac{4}{15}, \frac{7}{20}$

2. Write each list of fractions in descending order. Find a common denominator first, where necessary.

   a $\frac{2}{3}, \frac{3}{5}, \frac{11}{15}$ b $\frac{3}{4}, \frac{7}{16}, \frac{5}{8}$ c $\frac{13}{18}, \frac{2}{3}, \frac{7}{9}$

d $\frac{2}{3}, \frac{3}{5}, \frac{7}{10}$ **e** $\frac{4}{5}, \frac{7}{10}, \frac{11}{15}$ **f** $\frac{3}{5}, \frac{11}{15}, \frac{4}{9}$

g $\frac{3}{4}, \frac{5}{6}, \frac{4}{9}$ **h** $\frac{2}{3}, \frac{5}{6}, \frac{6}{7}$ **i** $\frac{13}{24}, \frac{3}{8}, \frac{7}{16}$

Reflect and reason

In **Q1**, why wasn't it possible to order the fractions by comparing the other two fractions to $\frac{1}{2}$?

In Purposeful practice 2, what method did you use to order the fractions?

⊠ Problem-solving practice

1 Use the numbers 1, 2, 3 and 4 to copy and complete each statement.

An example of a fraction 'more than $\frac{1}{2}$' is $\frac{\square}{\square}$.

An example of a fraction 'less than $\frac{1}{2}$' is $\frac{\square}{\square}$.

2 Three shops have these sales.

Shop A	Shop B	Shop C
$\frac{2}{5}$ off all prices	$\frac{1}{3}$ off everything	Clearance sale All stock $\frac{1}{2}$ price

    a Which shop is offering the best deal?

    b Which shop is offering the worst deal?

3 Are the fractions $\frac{7}{20}, \frac{3}{10}, \frac{2}{5}$ in descending order?
Give reasons for your answer.

4 Alfie has a bag of counters.
$\frac{1}{3}$ of the counters are red.
$\frac{2}{5}$ of the counters are blue.
$\frac{4}{15}$ of the counters are green.
Write the colour of the counters in order, starting with the least number of counters.

5 Phillip is asked to order the fractions $\frac{5}{6}, \frac{7}{12}, \frac{4}{5}$ in ascending order.

He says, 'The correct order is $\frac{4}{5}, \frac{5}{6}, \frac{7}{12}$ because 4, 5 and 7 are in ascending order.'

Phillip is incorrect. Explain why.

6 Four friends win a money prize and share the winnings.
Belle gets $\frac{1}{4}$ of the winnings.
Edward gets $\frac{1}{5}$ of the winnings.
Phil gets $\frac{13}{60}$ of the winnings.
Meera gets $\frac{1}{3}$ of the winnings.
Write the list of friends in the order of their winnings in descending order.

7 A list of fractions in ascending order is shown. Copy and complete it.

$\frac{1}{2}, \frac{\square}{5}, \frac{5}{\square}, \frac{\square}{8}, \frac{9}{10}$

8.2 Adding and subtracting fractions

Key point

- To add or subtract fractions, they must have a common denominator.

△ Purposeful practice 1

1 Work out

  a $\frac{1}{2} + \frac{1}{4}$ **b** $\frac{1}{4} + \frac{1}{8}$ **c** $\frac{1}{8} + \frac{1}{16}$ **d** $\frac{1}{5} + \frac{1}{10}$

  e $\frac{1}{10} + \frac{1}{20}$ **f** $\frac{1}{20} + \frac{1}{40}$ **g** $\frac{1}{7} + \frac{1}{14}$ **h** $\frac{1}{11} + \frac{1}{22}$

2 Work out

  a $\frac{2}{3} + \frac{1}{6}$ **b** $\frac{1}{4} + \frac{3}{8}$ **c** $\frac{4}{7} + \frac{1}{14}$ **d** $\frac{1}{20} + \frac{3}{10}$

  e $\frac{1}{9} + \frac{2}{3}$ **f** $\frac{2}{15} + \frac{2}{5}$ **g** $\frac{2}{5} + \frac{3}{20}$ **h** $\frac{5}{36} + \frac{2}{9}$

3 Work out each calculation, giving your answer as a fraction in its simplest form.

  a $\frac{1}{3} + \frac{1}{6}$ **b** $\frac{1}{6} + \frac{1}{12}$ **c** $\frac{1}{12} + \frac{1}{24}$ **d** $\frac{2}{5} + \frac{1}{10}$

  e $\frac{7}{10} + \frac{1}{20}$ **f** $\frac{1}{9} + \frac{5}{36}$ **g** $\frac{1}{18} + \frac{7}{36}$ **h** $\frac{1}{12} + \frac{7}{36}$

4 Work out each calculation, giving your answer as a mixed number.

  a $\frac{1}{2} + \frac{3}{4}$ **b** $\frac{1}{4} + \frac{7}{8}$ **c** $\frac{9}{10} + \frac{1}{5}$ **d** $\frac{5}{6} + \frac{1}{3}$

5 Work out each calculation, giving your answer as a mixed number and with any fractions in their simplest form.

  a $\frac{7}{10} + \frac{4}{5}$ **b** $\frac{5}{6} + \frac{2}{3}$ **c** $\frac{14}{15} + \frac{2}{5}$ **d** $\frac{3}{4} + \frac{5}{12}$

Reflect and reason

Alex writes $\frac{1}{4} + \frac{7}{8} = \frac{8}{12} = \frac{2}{3}$

What mistake has Alex made?

Copy these fractions of circles and use them to explain why Alex is wrong.

△ Purposeful practice 2

1 Work out

  a $\frac{1}{2} - \frac{1}{4}$ **b** $\frac{1}{4} - \frac{1}{8}$ **c** $\frac{1}{5} - \frac{1}{10}$ **d** $\frac{5}{6} - \frac{2}{3}$

  e $\frac{7}{9} - \frac{2}{3}$ **f** $\frac{8}{15} - \frac{2}{5}$ **g** $\frac{13}{16} - \frac{3}{4}$ **h** $\frac{2}{5} - \frac{3}{25}$

2 Work out each calculation, giving your answer as a fraction in its simplest form.

  a $\frac{3}{5} - \frac{1}{10}$ **b** $\frac{11}{12} - \frac{2}{3}$ **c** $\frac{13}{20} - \frac{2}{5}$ **d** $\frac{8}{9} - \frac{5}{36}$

Reflect and reason

How can you use Purposeful practice 1 **Q2** parts **e** and **f** to answer Purposeful practice 2 **Q1** parts **e** and **f**?

⚠ Purposeful practice 3

1 Work out each calculation, giving your answer as a fraction in its simplest form.

a $\frac{1}{3} + \frac{1}{4}$ **b** $\frac{1}{2} + \frac{2}{5}$ **c** $\frac{1}{3} + \frac{2}{5}$ **d** $\frac{1}{4} + \frac{3}{5}$

e $\frac{3}{8} - \frac{1}{12}$ **f** $\frac{4}{9} - \frac{1}{12}$ **g** $\frac{7}{10} + \frac{2}{15}$ **h** $\frac{3}{20} + \frac{4}{15}$

2 Work out each calculation, giving your answer as a mixed number and with any fractions in their simplest form.

a $\frac{1}{2} + \frac{2}{3}$ **b** $\frac{1}{2} + \frac{3}{5}$ **c** $\frac{1}{6} + \frac{8}{9}$ **d** $\frac{2}{3} + \frac{3}{4}$

e $\frac{3}{5} + \frac{2}{3}$ **f** $\frac{5}{8} + \frac{7}{12}$ **g** $\frac{5}{6} + \frac{3}{4}$ **h** $\frac{9}{10} + \frac{2}{15}$

Reflect and reason

What is the same and what is different about the method you used to work out the calculations in Purposeful practice 3, compared to Purposeful practice 1 and Purposeful practice 2?

⊠ Problem-solving practice

1 Eve makes two phone calls to a friend.

Her first call is for $\frac{1}{2}$ an hour.

Her second call is for $\frac{1}{5}$ of an hour.

What fraction of an hour does Eve spend on the phone to her friend?

2 Harley walks $\frac{3}{4}$ of a mile to school.

Isabella walks $\frac{2}{5}$ of a mile to school.

What is the difference in how far Harley and Isabella walk to school as a fraction of a mile?

3 Avinash includes this answer in his completed homework.

$\frac{7}{12} - \frac{1}{4} = \frac{6}{8}$

a Avinash is incorrect. Explain what he has done wrong.

b What is the correct answer to $\frac{7}{12} - \frac{1}{4}$?

4 Ashraf runs a café.

During one week, $\frac{3}{8}$ of the customers drink coffee and $\frac{2}{5}$ of the customers drink tea.

The rest of the customers drink cold drinks.

What fraction of the customers drink

a hot drinks **b** cold drinks?

5 Leila works out $\frac{5}{9} + \frac{1}{4}$.

She writes

$\frac{5}{9} + \frac{1}{4} = \frac{5}{36} + \frac{1}{36} = \frac{6}{36}$

Leila is incorrect. Explain why.

6 Write $\frac{3}{10}$ as the sum of two fractions with different denominators.

7 Copy and complete

$\frac{4}{5} + \frac{\square}{12} = 1\frac{13}{60}$

8.3 Multiplying fractions

Key points

- Finding a fraction of an integer is the same as multiplying a fraction and an integer.
- To multiply two fractions, multiply their numerators and multiply their denominators.
- Sometimes you can rearrange fractions so that they can be simplified before multiplying.

△ Purposeful practice 1

1 **a** $\frac{1}{3} \times 48$ **b** $\frac{1}{4} \times 48$ **c** $\frac{1}{6} \times 48$ **d** $\frac{1}{8} \times 48$

2 **a** $\frac{2}{3} \times 48$ **b** $\frac{3}{4} \times 48$ **c** $\frac{5}{6} \times 48$ **d** $\frac{7}{8} \times 48$

     e $\frac{11}{12} \times 48$ **f** $\frac{15}{16} \times 48$ **g** $\frac{23}{24} \times 48$ **h** $\frac{47}{48} \times 48$

Reflect and reason

How did your answers to **Q1** help you to answer **Q2** parts **a–d**?

△ Purposeful practice 2

1 Work out

    a $\frac{1}{3} \times \frac{1}{5}$ **b** $\frac{2}{3} \times \frac{1}{5}$ **c** $\frac{2}{3} \times \frac{1}{7}$ **d** $\frac{2}{5} \times \frac{1}{7}$

2 Work out each calculation, giving your answer as a fraction in its simplest form.

    a $\frac{1}{2} \times \frac{2}{3}$ **b** $\frac{1}{4} \times \frac{2}{3}$ **c** $\frac{1}{6} \times \frac{3}{4}$ **d** $\frac{1}{10} \times \frac{5}{6}$

    e $\frac{2}{9} \times \frac{3}{4}$ **f** $\frac{3}{10} \times \frac{5}{9}$ **g** $\frac{9}{10} \times \frac{2}{3}$ **h** $\frac{2}{3} \times \frac{15}{16}$

3 Work out

    a $\frac{3}{4} \times -\frac{5}{7}$ **b** $-\frac{3}{4} \times \frac{5}{7}$ **c** $\frac{3}{4} \times -\frac{3}{5}$ **d** $-\frac{3}{5} \times -\frac{2}{7}$

4 Work out each calculation, giving your answer as a fraction in its simplest form.

    a $-\frac{3}{4} \times \frac{2}{5}$ **b** $\frac{3}{8} \times -\frac{2}{9}$ **c** $-\frac{3}{4} \times -\frac{2}{9}$ **d** $-\frac{8}{15} \times -\frac{3}{4}$

Reflect and reason

When multiplying a fraction less than 1 by another fraction less than 1, do you always get an answer smaller than both of the original fractions? Give examples.

△ Purposeful practice 3

1 Copy and complete each calculation, where fractions are simplified in the working.

    a $\frac{9}{14} \times \frac{7}{12} = \frac{9 \times 7}{14 \times 12} = \frac{7 \times 9}{14 \times 12} = \frac{1 \times 3}{2 \times \square} = \frac{\square}{\square}$

    b $\frac{1}{12} \times \frac{2}{15} = \frac{1 \times 2}{12 \times 15} = \frac{2 \times 1}{12 \times 15} = \frac{1 \times 1}{\square \times 15} = \frac{\square}{\square}$

    c $\frac{5}{18} \times \frac{9}{11} = \frac{5 \times 9}{18 \times 11} = \frac{9 \times 5}{18 \times 11} = \frac{1 \times \square}{\square \times 11} = \frac{\square}{\square}$

d $\dfrac{3}{16} \times \dfrac{4}{9} = \dfrac{3 \times 4}{16 \times 9} = \dfrac{4 \times 3}{16 \times 9} = \dfrac{\square \times \square}{\square \times \square} = \dfrac{\square}{\square}$

2 Use the method shown in **Q1** to work out

a $\dfrac{3}{22} \times \dfrac{11}{12}$ **b** $\dfrac{3}{15} \times \dfrac{5}{24}$ **c** $\dfrac{5}{36} \times \dfrac{9}{10}$ **d** $\dfrac{7}{40} \times \dfrac{8}{21}$

e $\dfrac{3}{32} \times \dfrac{4}{9}$ **f** $\dfrac{9}{28} \times \dfrac{7}{18}$ **g** $\dfrac{5}{42} \times \dfrac{7}{20}$ **h** $\dfrac{9}{88} \times \dfrac{11}{27}$

3 Work out

a $\dfrac{15}{24} \times \dfrac{3}{25}$ **b** $\dfrac{3}{35} \times \dfrac{14}{27}$ **c** $\dfrac{18}{77} \times \dfrac{22}{45}$ **d** $\dfrac{28}{45} \times \dfrac{20}{49}$

Reflect and reason

Why is it sometimes useful to simplify fractions in the working when multiplying fractions?

⊠ Problem-solving practice

1 There are 200 students in Year 8.

$\dfrac{3}{4}$ of the students walk to school.

$\dfrac{1}{5}$ of the students travel to school by car.

The rest of the students travel by bus.

a How many students travel to school by car?

b How many students walk to school?

c How many students travel to school by bus?

2 Use the symbols '<', '=' or '>' to compare

a $\dfrac{4}{5} \times 30$ and $\dfrac{3}{4} \times 32$ **b** $\dfrac{5}{12} \times 60$ and $\dfrac{3}{10} \times 80$

3 $\dfrac{3}{4}$ of a number is 54. What is the number?

4 Work out the area of the rectangle.
Give your answer as a fraction in m².

$\dfrac{5}{6}$ m

$\dfrac{1}{2}$ m

5 Mark is buying a TV that costs £600.
The TV is on sale in two different shops.
Which shop should Mark buy his TV from? Explain why.

Shop A	**Shop B**
$\frac{1}{4}$ off all prices	$\frac{1}{3}$ off TVs

6 Work out each missing fraction.

a $\dfrac{4}{5} \times \dfrac{\square}{\square} = \dfrac{12}{35}$ **b** $\dfrac{\square}{\square} \times -\dfrac{1}{3} = \dfrac{2}{15}$

7 On an exam paper, a 2-mark question is:

'Work out $\dfrac{15}{16} \times \dfrac{8}{21}$ and write your answer in its simplest form.'

Grant writes

$\dfrac{15}{16} \times \dfrac{8}{21} = \dfrac{15 \times 8}{16 \times 21} = \dfrac{8 \times 15}{16 \times 21} = \dfrac{4 \times 5}{8 \times 7} = \dfrac{20}{56}$

a Grant only gets 1 out of the 2 marks awarded for this question. Explain why.

b What is the correct answer?

8.4 Dividing fractions

Key points

- You can write integers (whole numbers) as fractions with a denominator of 1. Dividing by 1 does not change the number. For example, $\frac{3}{1} = 3$.
- The reciprocal of a fraction is the 'upside down' fraction, for example, the reciprocal of $\frac{2}{3}$ is $\frac{3}{2}$.
- Dividing by a fraction is the same as multiplying by its reciprocal.
- An improper fraction is a fraction in which the numerator is greater than or equal to the denominator.

△ Purposeful practice 1

1 Write the reciprocal of these improper and proper fractions.

  a $\frac{3}{2}$ **b** $\frac{4}{3}$ **c** $\frac{5}{2}$ **d** $\frac{5}{3}$ **e** $\frac{2}{3}$ **f** $\frac{3}{4}$ **g** $\frac{2}{5}$ **h** $\frac{3}{5}$

2 Write the reciprocal of these unit fractions and integers.

  a $\frac{1}{6}$ **b** $\frac{1}{7}$ **c** $\frac{1}{8}$ **d** $\frac{1}{9}$ **e** 4   **f** 14   **g** 24   **h** 108

Reflect and reason

Copy and complete the sentence four times using words from these boxes.

| an improper fraction | | a proper fraction | | a unit fraction | | an integer |

The reciprocal of _____ is _____.

△ Purposeful practice 2

Work out

1 **a** $2 \div \frac{1}{2}$ **b** $2 \div \frac{1}{3}$ **c** $3 \div \frac{1}{2}$ **d** $3 \div \frac{1}{3}$

  e $3 \div \frac{1}{4}$ **f** $4 \div \frac{1}{3}$ **g** $4 \div \frac{1}{4}$ **h** $5 \div \frac{1}{5}$

2 **a** $12 \div \frac{1}{5}$ **b** $12 \div \frac{2}{5}$ **c** $12 \div \frac{3}{5}$ **d** $12 \div \frac{4}{5}$

  e $10 \div \frac{1}{9}$ **f** $10 \div \frac{2}{9}$ **g** $10 \div \frac{3}{9}$ **h** $10 \div \frac{5}{9}$

Reflect and reason

What type of numbers are the answers to calculations in **Q1** parts **a**, **d**, **g**, and **h**?
Explain why you get these numbers.
Do you get these numbers when the numerator of the fraction is not 1? Explain.

△ Purposeful practice 3

1 Work out each calculation. Give your answers as proper or improper fractions and in their simplest form, where necessary.

  a $\frac{1}{3} \div \frac{1}{2}$ **b** $\frac{3}{7} \div \frac{3}{5}$ **c** $\frac{4}{9} \div \frac{4}{5}$ **d** $\frac{5}{13} \div \frac{5}{11}$

  e $\frac{1}{2} \div \frac{1}{3}$ **f** $\frac{3}{5} \div \frac{3}{7}$ **g** $\frac{4}{5} \div \frac{4}{9}$ **h** $\frac{5}{11} \div \frac{5}{13}$

2 Work out

a $\frac{2}{5} \div \frac{3}{4}$ **b** $\frac{2}{3} \div \frac{5}{7}$ **c** $\frac{2}{9} \div \frac{3}{4}$ **d** $\frac{4}{9} \div \frac{5}{7}$

3 Work out each calculation, giving your answer in its simplest form.

a $\frac{2}{3} \div \frac{5}{6}$ **b** $\frac{3}{4} \div \frac{7}{8}$ **c** $\frac{3}{10} \div \frac{2}{5}$ **d** $\frac{5}{12} \div \frac{2}{3}$

e $\frac{2}{9} \div \frac{4}{11}$ **f** $\frac{6}{25} \div \frac{3}{5}$ **g** $\frac{3}{13} \div \frac{9}{26}$ **h** $\frac{7}{9} \div \frac{14}{15}$

4 Work out each calculation, giving your answer as a mixed number in its simplest form.

a $\frac{2}{3} \div \frac{5}{8}$ **b** $\frac{3}{4} \div \frac{7}{11}$ **c** $\frac{5}{9} \div \frac{3}{8}$ **d** $\frac{5}{6} \div \frac{3}{4}$

Reflect and reason

Look at the calculations and answers in **Q1** parts **a–d** and **Q1** parts **e–h**. What do you notice about dividing one fraction by another where the numerators are the same?

Did you use a different method for **Q3** parts **a–d** and **Q3** parts **e–h**? If so, explain how your method for **Q3** parts **e–h** made the calculations easier.

⊠ Problem-solving practice

1 **a** Work out the reciprocal of $\frac{3}{7}$.

   b Multiply $\frac{3}{7}$ by its reciprocal. Write your answer in its simplest form.

   c Work out the reciprocal of 8.

   d Multiply 8 by its reciprocal. Write your answer in its simplest form.

   e Based on your answers to parts **b** and **d**, what is the value of a fraction or integer multiplied by its reciprocal?

   f Choose your own fractions and integers to multiply by their reciprocals to check if your answer to part **e** works for other fractions and integers.

2 Copy and complete, writing your answer in is simplest form: $3 \div \dfrac{\square}{\square} = 12$

3 An 8 m long piece of ribbon is cut into strips of length $\frac{2}{5}$ m.

   How many $\frac{2}{5}$ m strips of ribbon are there?

4 Charlotte spends $\frac{5}{6}$ of an hour walking home. She shares her time equally between talking to a friend and talking to her mum whilst walking home.

   What fraction of an hour does Charlotte spend talking to her friend?

5 Three students are asked to work out $\frac{5}{9} \div \frac{3}{4}$.

   Ella writes $\dfrac{5}{9} \div \dfrac{3}{4} = \dfrac{9}{5} \times \dfrac{4}{3} = \dfrac{9 \times 4}{5 \times 3} = \dfrac{36}{15}$

   Layla writes $\dfrac{5}{9} \div \dfrac{3}{4} = \dfrac{5}{9} \times \dfrac{4}{3} = \dfrac{5 \times 4}{9 \times 3} = \dfrac{20}{27}$

   Ebo writes $\dfrac{5}{9} \div \dfrac{3}{4} = \dfrac{5 \div 3}{9 \div 4} = \dfrac{1.6666\ldots}{2.25}$

   Who is correct? Explain why.

6 Callum says, 'Division always makes the number you start with smaller.'
   Use these calculations to explain whether or not Callum is correct.

$20 \div 5$		$20 \div 1$		$20 \div \frac{1}{5}$		$\frac{1}{20} \div \frac{1}{5}$

Key points

- You can add or subtract mixed numbers by adding or subtracting the whole number first, then adding or subtracting the fraction parts.
- It can be easier to write mixed numbers as improper fractions before subtracting.
- Write mixed numbers as improper fractions before multiplying or dividing.

△ Purposeful practice 1

Work out these calculations. Give your answers in their simplest form, where necessary.

1 a $1\frac{1}{5} + 2\frac{2}{5}$ **b** $1\frac{1}{5} + 2\frac{4}{5}$ **c** $1\frac{2}{5} + 2\frac{4}{5}$ **d** $4\frac{3}{5} + 2\frac{4}{5}$

2 a $1\frac{2}{5} + 2\frac{3}{10}$ **b** $1\frac{2}{5} + 2\frac{6}{10}$ **c** $1\frac{4}{5} + 2\frac{7}{10}$ **d** $4\frac{4}{5} + 2\frac{7}{10}$

3 a $1\frac{1}{4} + 2\frac{1}{10}$ **b** $1\frac{1}{4} + 2\frac{3}{10}$ **c** $1\frac{3}{4} + 2\frac{3}{10}$ **d** $4\frac{3}{4} + 2\frac{3}{10}$

Reflect and reason

Rebecca and David are working out $1\frac{1}{6} + 3\frac{2}{3}$. The start of their working is shown.

Rebecca

$$1\frac{1}{6} + 3\frac{2}{3} = 1 + 3 + \frac{1}{6} + \frac{2}{3}$$
$$= 1 + 3 + \frac{1}{6} + \frac{4}{6}$$
$$= 4 + \frac{5}{6}$$

David

$$1\frac{1}{6} + 3\frac{2}{3} = \frac{7}{6} + \frac{11}{3}$$
$$= \frac{7}{6} + \frac{22}{6}$$

Copy and complete each of their working to show they get the same answer.

Use each of their methods to work out $1\frac{5}{6} + 3\frac{2}{3}$. Which method do you prefer? Explain.

△ Purposeful practice 2

Work out each calculation, giving your answer as a mixed number and in its simplest form, where necessary.

1 a $3\frac{7}{9} - 1\frac{5}{9}$ **b** $3\frac{7}{9} - 1\frac{8}{9}$ **c** $3\frac{4}{9} - 1\frac{5}{9}$ **d** $3\frac{4}{9} - 1\frac{7}{9}$

2 a $1\frac{1}{9} - 1\frac{1}{18}$ **b** $1\frac{4}{9} - 1\frac{1}{18}$ **c** $2\frac{2}{9} - 1\frac{11}{18}$ **d** $2\frac{1}{18} - 1\frac{7}{9}$

3 a $5\frac{3}{4} - 3\frac{1}{2}$ **b** $5\frac{3}{4} - 3\frac{1}{8}$ **c** $5\frac{1}{8} - 3\frac{3}{4}$ **d** $5\frac{3}{8} - 3\frac{3}{4}$

Reflect and reason

Here is Isla's working for $6\frac{1}{5} - 1\frac{7}{10}$.

$$6\frac{1}{5} - 1\frac{7}{10} = 6 - 1 - \frac{1}{5} - \frac{7}{10}$$
$$= 5 - \frac{2}{10} - \frac{7}{10}$$
$$= 5 - \frac{9}{10}$$
$$= 4\frac{1}{10}$$

Write the mixed numbers as improper fractions and then subtract to check Isla's working. What did Isla do wrong?

△ Purposeful practice 3

Work out each calculation, giving your answer as an integer, a mixed number or a fraction in its simplest form.

1 a $4\frac{1}{3} \times \frac{1}{2}$ **b** $4\frac{1}{3} \times 2$ **c** $4\frac{1}{3} \times 2\frac{1}{2}$ **d** $4\frac{1}{2} \times 2\frac{1}{3}$

     e $10\frac{1}{2} \times 3\frac{1}{7}$ **f** $10\frac{1}{7} \times 3\frac{1}{2}$ **g** $10\frac{2}{7} \times 2\frac{1}{3}$ **h** $10\frac{2}{7} \times 2\frac{1}{2}$

2 a $7\frac{1}{2} \div 3$ **b** $5\frac{1}{3} \div 4$ **c** $5\frac{1}{3} \div \frac{3}{4}$ **d** $8\frac{1}{3} \div \frac{5}{9}$

     e $8\frac{1}{3} \div 5\frac{5}{9}$ **f** $5\frac{5}{9} \div 2\frac{1}{2}$ **g** $9\frac{1}{11} \div 2\frac{1}{2}$ **h** $6\frac{2}{3} \div 9\frac{1}{11}$

Reflect and reason

Write one thing that is the same and one thing that is different when multiplying and when dividing a mixed number by a mixed number.

⊠ Problem-solving practice

1 Paul cycled $5\frac{1}{3}$ miles.

Jane cycled $8\frac{4}{5}$ miles. How much further did Jane cycle?

2 Lorna makes green paint by mixing $2\frac{3}{10}$ litres of yellow paint and $1\frac{1}{4}$ litres of blue paint.
How many litres of green paint does Lorna make?

3 Work out the area of the rectangle. Give your answer as a mixed number in m².

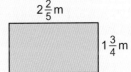

4 Here is an addition pyramid.
The number in any brick is the sum of the numbers in the two bricks below.
Copy and complete the addition pyramid.

5 Copy and complete the multiplication grid.

×	$1\frac{1}{2}$		$2\frac{1}{3}$
			$3\frac{4}{15}$
$1\frac{3}{8}$		$3\frac{3}{32}$	
	$3\frac{1}{2}$		

6 Max works out $3\frac{1}{5} \times 1\frac{1}{4}$.
He writes

$3 \times 1 = 3$ and $\frac{1}{5} \times \frac{1}{4} = \frac{1}{20}$

So $3\frac{1}{5} \times 1\frac{1}{4} = 3\frac{1}{20}$

The answer $3\frac{1}{20}$ is wrong.

     a What mistake has Max made?
     b What is the correct answer?

9.1 Direct proportion on graphs

Key point

When two quantities are in direct proportion,
- plotting them as a graph gives a straight line through (0, 0)
- when one variable is zero, the other variable is also zero
- when one variable doubles, so does the other

△ Purposeful practice 1

Which of these graphs show two quantities in direct proportion to each other?

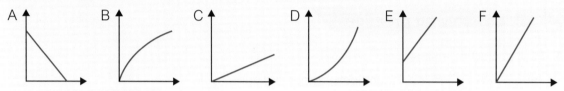

Reflect and reason

Dan says, 'All straight-line graphs show quantities in direct proportion to each other.'
Is Dan correct? Explain.

△ Purposeful practice 2

The graphs show the price of coffee beans sold by mass (in grams) in a shop and online.

1 a Saira buys 200 g of coffee beans in a shop.
      How much does she pay?
   b How many grams of coffee beans can she buy in a shop
      i for £7.50
      ii for £3
      iii with a £20 note?

2 Is the price directly proportional to the mass of coffee beans
   a in the shop
   b online?
   Explain your answers.

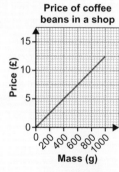

Price of coffee beans in a shop

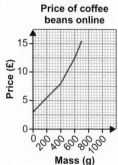

Price of coffee beans online

Reflect and reason

When two quantities are in direct proportion, what methods can you use to work out values not shown on a graph (for example, in **Q1b iii**)?

Are these quantities in direct proportion? Explain and show your working.

1

Feet	Centimetres
1	30.48
2	60.96
3	91.44
4	121.92

2

Hours worked	Pay (£)
2	24
3	36
4	48
5	75

Reflect and reason

Angelo only looked at the first three rows of data in each table.

He says, 'This is enough to decide if the quantities are in direct proportion.'

Is Angelo correct? Explain.

⊠ **Problem-solving practice**

1 The graph shows how much an electrician charges for jobs.

   a Use the graph to work out how much the electrician charges for a job that takes

      i 3 hours   **ii** 8 hours

   b The electrician charges £395 for a job.
      How long did the job take?

   c Is the amount charged by this electrician directly proportional to the number of hours spent on a job? Explain why.

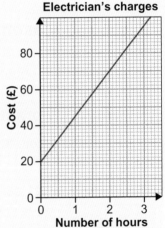

Electrician's charges

2 This graph can be used for converting between kilograms (kg) and pounds (lb).

   a Use the graph to determine which is greater: 8 kg or 15 lb.

   b Jessica weighs her dog every week and records the measurement.
      One week the scales say 48 kg. Jessica prefers lbs so she changes the settings, and the next week the scales say 106 lb.
      Did the dog gain or lose weight? Explain.

   c Are kilograms and pounds in direct proportion? Explain why or why not.

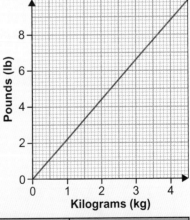

Conversion between pounds and kilograms

3 The table shows the number of years after purchase and the value of an artwork.
Daniel says, 'The number of years after purchase and value of the artwork are in direct proportion, because $1 \times 2 = 2$ and $5000 \times 2 = 10000$, so both variables double.'

Daniel is incorrect. Explain why.

Number of years	Value of artwork (£)
1	5000
2	10000
3	16000
6	30000

Key points

- The steepness of a line or graph is called the gradient.
- To find the gradient, work out how many units the line or graph goes up for every one unit across to the right. If the line goes down, the gradient is negative.

⚠ Purposeful practice 1

1 Copy and complete the table of values for
  a $y = x + 1$　　　　　**b** $y = x + 3$
  c $y = 2x + 1$　　　　　**d** $y = 2x + 3$

x	-2	-1	0	1	2
y					

2 Plot the graphs from **Q1** parts **a–d** on a single grid with both axes from -8 to 8. Label each graph with its equation.

Reflect and reason

Which graphs in **Q1** have the same gradient?

What do you notice about the equations of graphs with the same gradient?

⚠ Purposeful practice 2

1 Copy and complete the table of values in Purposeful practice 1 **Q1** for
  a $y = -x + 1$　　　**b** $y = -x + 3$　　　**c** $y = -2x + 1$　　　**d** $y = -2x + 3$

2 Plot graphs for **Q1** parts **a–d** on a single grid with both axes from -8 to 8. Label each graph with its equation.

Reflect and reason

Compare graphs in Purposeful practice 1 **Q1** parts **a** and **b** with the graphs in Purposeful practice 2 **Q1** parts **a** and **b**.

What do you notice about the graphs? And what do you notice about their equations?

⚠ Purposeful practice 3

Work out the gradient of each line in the diagrams.

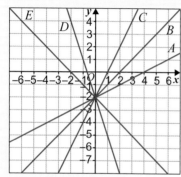
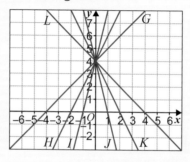

Reflect and reason

Which line is the least steep? And which is the most steep?

1 Reuben is asked to draw a table of values for $y = -2x + 5$ and plot its graph.
Reuben's table and graph are shown.

x	-2	-1	0	1	2
y	1	3	5	3	1

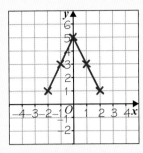

Reuben is incorrect.

  a How should Reuben know from his graph that he is incorrect?

  b Draw the correct graph of $y = -2x + 5$ between $x = -2$ and $x = 2$.

2 **a** Copy and complete the table of values for

    i $y = x$

    ii $y = -2x$

x	-2	-1	0	1	2
y					

  b Plot the graphs for parts **i** and **ii** on a single grid with both axes from –6 to 6.
Label each graph with its equation.

  c Work out the gradient of each graph.

3 **a** Sort the lines into groups of equal gradient.

  b There is one group that has only one line in it.
Copy the grid and this line.
Draw another line that would fit into this group.

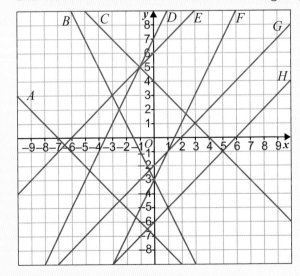

4 **a** Draw a grid with both axes from -5 to 5.
Draw and label a line with gradient 1.

  b On the same grid draw and label a line with gradient -1.

  c On the same grid draw and label a line with gradient 2.

  d On the same grid draw and label a line with gradient -2.

Key points

- The y-intercept is where a line or graph crosses the y-axis.
- A linear equation generates a straight line (linear) graph.
  The equation for a straight line graph can be written as $y = mx + c$ where m is the gradient and c is the y-intercept.

△ Purposeful practice 1

1 a Copy and complete the table of values for

    i $y = 3x - 3$ **ii** $y = 3x - 2$ **iii** $y = 3x - 1$ **iv** $y = 3x + 2$

x	-2	-1	0	1	2
y					

  b Plot the graphs for each equation in part **a** on a single grid, with both axes from −9 to 9. Label each graph.

2 a Copy and complete the table of values for

    i $y = -x$ **ii** $y = -x + 1$ **iii** $y = -2x + 1$ **iv** $y = -3x + 1$

x	-2	-1	0	1	2
y					

  b Plot graphs for each equation in part **a**, on a single grid with both axes from −10 to 10. Label each graph.

Reflect and reason

What is the same and what is different about the equations and graphs in **Q1**?

What is the same and what is different about the equations and graphs in **Q2** parts **i–iii**?

△ Purposeful practice 2

Match each graph to its equation.

1 $y = x + 1$ **2** $y = 4x - 2$

3 $y = \frac{1}{2}x - 2$ **4** $y = -x + 1$

5 $y = -4x - 2$ **6** $y = -x - 1$

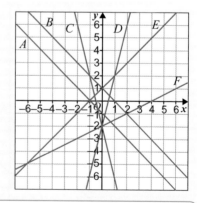

Reflect and reason

Antony says, 'To answer this question, I looked at where each graph crossed the y-axis first then matched its gradient.'

Judith says, 'To answer this question, I looked at graphs with positive gradients first and compared their steepness.'

Whose first step do you prefer? Explain why.

What was your first step to answer this question?

1 Copy and complete the table.

Equation	Gradient	y-intercept
$y = x + 5$	1	5
$y = x \square \square$		-5
$y = -2x + 3$		
$y = \square x \square \square$	-3	2
$y = \square x \square \square$	4	-5
	5	2

2 Megan says, 'The lines with equations $y = 3x - 1$ and $y = x - 3$ are parallel as they each have a 3 in the equation.'
Is Megan correct? Explain.

3 Do the lines with equations $y = 2x - 5$ and $y = 2x + 5$ have the same y-intercept?
Give a reason for your answer.

4 The graph shows the line $y = 2x - 3$.

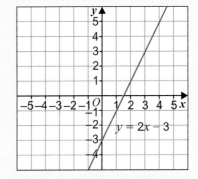

   a Copy the graph.
      Write the equations of four other lines which are
      parallel to $y = 2x - 3$.
      Plot and label them on the graph.

   b Write the equation of two other lines with the same
      y-intercept as $y = 2x - 3$.
      Plot and label them on the graph.

5 The graph shows two lines.

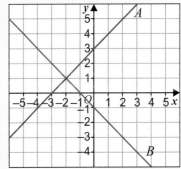

   a Write the equation of each line.
   b The two lines form two sides of a square.
      Write the equations of two lines that could complete
      the square.

6 The equations of eight lines A–H are shown.

A: $y = 5x - 1$ B: $y = -5x + 1$ C: $y = -3x - 2$ D: $y = 2x - 1$

E: $y = 3x + 2$ F: $y = 4x - 1$ G: $y = 3x - 3$ H: $y = x + 3$

   a Which equations have the same gradient? Explain why.
   b Which equations have the same y-intercept? Explain why.
   c Write an equation for a line parallel to line B.
   d Write an equation with the same y-intercept as line C.

10 Percentages, decimals and fractions

10.1 Fractions and decimals

Key points

- A terminating decimal ends after a definite number of digits, for example 0.22 or 0.519
- The line in a fraction means 'divide by'. You can use written division to write fractions as decimals. For example, to write $\frac{3}{8}$ as a decimal, work out $8\overline{)3}$.
- A recurring decimal contains a digit, or sequence of digits, which repeats itself forever.
- In a recurring decimal, a dot over a digit shows it recurs; a dot over the beginning and end of a sequence shows that the sequence recurs. For example, $0.\dot{7} = 0.777\,777...$, $0.1\dot{7} = 0.177\,7777...$, $0.\dot{1}0\dot{7} = 0.107\,107\,107...$
- A fraction of an hour is $\frac{\square}{60}$. For example, 45 minutes is $\frac{45}{60} = \frac{3}{4} = 0.75$ hours.

⚠ Purposeful practice 1

1 Write each fraction as a decimal.

  a $\frac{3}{1000}$ **b** $\frac{30}{1000}$ **c** $\frac{303}{1000}$ **d** $\frac{33}{1000}$

  e $\frac{330}{1000}$ **f** $\frac{33}{10000}$ **g** $\frac{303}{10000}$ **h** $\frac{330}{10000}$

2 Write each decimal as a fraction.

  a 0.09   **b** 0.009   **c** 0.0009   **d** 0.099   **e** 0.0099   **f** 0.0999

3 Write each decimal as a fraction in its simplest form.

  a 0.04   **b** 0.004   **c** 0.0004   **d** 0.044   **e** 0.0044   **f** 0.0444

Reflect and reason

Simon says, 'The decimal in **Q2f** is a recurring decimal.'

Is he correct? Explain.

⚠ Purposeful practice 2

1 Write each number of sixteenths as a terminating decimal.
Simplify first if it helps you.

  a $\frac{1}{16}$ **b** $\frac{2}{16}$ **c** $\frac{3}{16}$ **d** $\frac{4}{16}$ **e** $\frac{5}{16}$ **f** $\frac{6}{16}$ **g** $\frac{7}{16}$ **h** $\frac{8}{16}$

2 Write each fraction as a recurring decimal, using dot notation.

  a $\frac{1}{3}$ **b** $\frac{2}{3}$ **c** $\frac{1}{11}$ **d** $\frac{2}{11}$ **e** $\frac{3}{11}$ **f** $\frac{4}{11}$ **g** $\frac{5}{11}$ **h** $\frac{6}{11}$

Reflect and reason

How could you use the answer to **Q2a** to work out the answer to **Q2b**?

How could you use the answer to **Q2c** to work out the answers to **Q2** parts **d–h**?

Purposeful practice 3

1 Write these lengths of time as terminating decimals.

   a 2 hours 3 minutes   **b** 2 hours 6 minutes   **c** 2 hours 9 minutes

   d 2 hours 12 minutes   **e** 2 hours 15 minutes   **f** 2 hours 18 minutes

2 Write these lengths of time as recurring decimals.

   a 2 hours 2 minutes   **b** 2 hours 4 minutes   **c** 2 hours 8 minutes

> ### Reflect and reason
> When are fractions of hours terminating decimals?

Problem-solving practice

1 State whether each statement is true or false.
Give reasons for your answers.

   a $\dfrac{7}{1000} = 0.0007$ **b** $\dfrac{702}{10\,000} = 0.0702$ **c** $0.006 = \dfrac{3}{500}$

2 **a** Sort these fractions into those that convert to terminating decimals and those that convert to recurring decimals.
Use division to help you decide if you are not sure.

$\dfrac{1}{2}$	$\dfrac{1}{3}$	$\dfrac{1}{4}$	$\dfrac{1}{5}$	$\dfrac{1}{6}$	$\dfrac{1}{7}$	$\dfrac{1}{8}$	$\dfrac{1}{9}$	$\dfrac{1}{10}$	$\dfrac{1}{11}$	$\dfrac{1}{12}$

   b How do you know if a fraction converts to a terminating or recurring decimal?

3 Sian buys 8 raffle tickets and Brody buys 5 raffle tickets.
1000 raffle tickets are sold in total.

   a What fraction of the raffle tickets does   **i** Sian buy   **ii** Brody buy?
Give your answers in their simplest form.

   b Write your answers to part **a** as decimals.

4 Aisha says, 'Multiplying by 0.3 is the same as multiplying by $\frac{1}{3}$.'
Is Aisha correct? Explain why.

5 Gareth uses his calculator to work out the answer to a time calculation in hours.
The calculator display shows the answer

   `0.55`

Gareth writes the answer as 55 minutes.

   a Explain why Gareth is wrong.

   b What answer should Gareth have written down in minutes?

6 Sort these times into those that produce a terminating decimal and those that produce a recurring decimal when converted to hours.
Explain how you decided.

   A: 4 hours 36 minutes   B: 4 hours 20 minutes   C: 4 hours 50 minutes

   D: 4 hours 51 minutes   E: 4 hours 57 minutes   F: 4 hours 25 minutes

7 Dan spends $1\frac{3}{4}$ hours completing his homework.
Lucy spends 1 hour and 44 minutes completing her homework.
Abdul spends 1.7 hours completing his homework.
Who spent the longest amount of time on homework? Explain why.

10.2 Equivalent proportions

Key points

- A positive mixed number is greater than 1, so the decimal equivalent is greater than 1 and the percentage equivalent is greater than 100%. For example, $1\frac{3}{4} = 1.75 = 175\%$.
- A proportion of a whole can be written as a fraction, decimal or percentage.
- Sometimes you might need to use a denominator of 1000 when you convert between fractions, decimals and percentages.

△ Purposeful practice 1

1 Write these fractions and mixed numbers as decimals.

   a $\frac{1}{5}$ **b** $1\frac{1}{5}$ **c** $27\frac{1}{5}$ **d** $27\frac{3}{5}$ **e** $\frac{1}{25}$ **f** $32\frac{1}{25}$ **g** $32\frac{2}{25}$ **h** $32\frac{4}{25}$

2 Write these fractions and mixed numbers as percentages.

   a $\frac{1}{5}$ **b** $1\frac{1}{5}$ **c** $\frac{1}{25}$ **d** $1\frac{1}{25}$ **e** $2\frac{1}{25}$ **f** $2\frac{4}{25}$ **g** $2\frac{1}{20}$ **h** $2\frac{3}{20}$

3 Write these percentages as mixed numbers with fractions in their simplest form.

   a 110%   **b** 130%   **c** 170%   **d** 270%   **e** 105%

   f 175%   **g** 135%   **h** 235%   **i** 102%   **j** 114%

Reflect and reason

Holly uses this method to write mixed numbers as decimals.
First she writes the mixed number as an improper fraction. $3\frac{3}{50} = \frac{153}{50} \xrightarrow{\times 2} \frac{306}{100} = 3.06$
Is this a good method? Explain.

Do you have to convert to improper fractions to write a mixed number as a decimal? If not, show a different method.

When does it help to convert mixed numbers to improper fractions?

△ Purposeful practice 2

1 Write these fractions as decimals and percentages.

   a $\frac{1}{40}$ **b** $\frac{2}{40}$ **c** $\frac{3}{40}$ **d** $\frac{4}{40}$ **e** $\frac{5}{40}$ **f** $\frac{6}{40}$ **g** $\frac{7}{40}$ **h** $\frac{8}{40}$

2 Write these fractions as decimals and percentages.

   a $\frac{1}{125}$ **b** $\frac{2}{125}$ **c** $\frac{3}{125}$ **d** $\frac{3}{250}$ **e** $\frac{4}{250}$ **f** $\frac{5}{250}$ **g** $\frac{6}{500}$ **h** $\frac{7}{500}$

3 Write these proportions of Year 8 students as percentages.

   a 2 out of 200 Year 8 students play the trumpet.

   b 1 out of 200 Year 8 students rides a unicycle.

   c 3 out of 200 Year 8 students speak Mandarin.

   d 30 out of 200 Year 8 students play basketball.

   e 90 out of 200 Year 8 students walk to school.

Reflect and reason

Why are these answers the same: **Q2b** and **Q2e**; **Q2d** and **Q2g**?

⚠ Purposeful practice 3

1 Write these percentages as decimals.

   a 125%   **b** 225%   **c** 250%   **d** 1250%

2 Write these percentages as decimals and fractions in their simplest form.

   a 2.1%   **b** 4.2%   **c** 8.4%   **d** 10.5%   **e** 37.5%   **f** 62.5%   **g** 87.5%

Reflect and reason

Jon writes

13.5% is the decimal 1.35 and the fraction $\frac{135}{100} = \frac{27}{20} = 1\frac{7}{20}$

What mistake has Jon made? What is the correct answer?

⊠ Problem-solving practice

1 Caroline is asked to write $3\frac{1}{2}$ as a percentage.
   She writes
   $3\frac{1}{2} = 3.5\%$
   Is Caroline correct? Explain.

2 Which decimal is equivalent to 2510%?

   A 0.251   B 2.51   C 25.1   D 251.0

3 Which is smaller, $2\frac{3}{5}$ or 255%?
   Give a reason for your answer.

4 Seth, Katie and Esme sit a test.
   The total for the test is 80 marks.
   Seth achieves 54 marks.
   Katie achieves $\frac{5}{8}$ of 80 marks.
   Esme achieves 65% of 80 marks.
   Who achieves the highest mark?
   You must show all your working.

5 Farrah sits three science tests.
   Test A is 100 marks and tests B and C are 75 marks each.
   Farrah scores 64 marks in test A, 52 marks in test B and 45 marks in test C.
   All three test scores are combined to give an overall percentage.
   a What is Farrah's percentage for all three tests?
   b In which of the three tests did Farrah score the highest percentage?

6 Write these values in order, starting with the smallest.

   $\boxed{23\frac{4}{5}}$ $\boxed{23.45}$ $\boxed{234.5\%}$

7 A dealer makes a profit of 175% on one particular item.
   a Write the profit as a decimal.
   b Write the profit as a fraction in its simplest form.
   Another dealer makes a profit of 115% on a similar item.
   Dave writes
   $115\% = 11.5 = 11\frac{1}{2}$
   c Dave is incorrect. Explain why.

- To express one amount as a fraction or percentage of another, they must be in the same units.
- To increase an amount by a percentage, you can find the percentage of the amount, then add it to the original amount.
- To decrease an amount by a percentage, you can find the percentage of the amount, then subtract it from the original amount.
- Interest is money charged for borrowing or earned for saving. Simple interest is interest calculated only on the original amount of money. It is the same amount each year.

⚠ Purposeful practice 1

1 Write each amount in ml as a proportion of the amount in litres.
   Give your answer as a percentage.
   a 500 ml, 1 litre **b** 250 ml, 1 litre **c** 100 ml, 1 litre **d** 350 ml, 1 litre
   e 350 ml, $\frac{1}{2}$ litre **f** 120 ml, $\frac{1}{2}$ litre **g** 120 ml, $\frac{1}{4}$ litre **h** 85 ml, $\frac{1}{4}$ litre

2 Write each amount in grams (g) as a proportion of the amount in kilograms (kg).
   Give your answer as a percentage.
   a 250 g, 1 kg **b** 125 g, 1 kg **c** 375 g, 1 kg **d** 375 g, $\frac{1}{2}$ kg
   e 75 g, $\frac{1}{4}$ kg **f** 150 g, $\frac{1}{4}$ kg **g** 300 g, $\frac{1}{4}$ kg **h** 300 g, $\frac{1}{8}$ kg

3 Write each amount in pence (p) as a proportion of the amount in pounds (£).
   Give your answer as a percentage.
   a 50p, £2 **b** 52p, £2 **c** 52p, £4 **d** 52p, £5
   e 55p, £5 **f** 55p, £2.50 **g** 55p, £1.25 **h** 55p, £0.50

Reflect and reason
What do you notice about your answers to **Q2** parts **g** and **h**, and **Q3** parts **f** and **g**? Explain.

⚠ Purposeful practice 2

1 Work out each cost plus 20% VAT.
   a £10 **b** £20 **c** £30 **d** £40 **e** £12 **f** £24 **g** £36 **h** £48

2 Work out
   i 10% of each mass   **ii** the mass decreased by 10%
   a 600 g **b** 300 g **c** 150 g **d** 75 g

3 For each mass in **Q2**, work out
   i 5% of the mass   **ii** the mass decreased by 5%
   iii 15% of the mass   **iv** the mass decreased by 15%

Reflect and reason
What do you notice about the amount you were subtracting for a decrease of 5%, then 10%, then 15% of each mass?
Predict 600 g decreased by 20%. Write a calculation to check your prediction.

△ Purposeful practice 3

1 A bank offers 1% simple interest on its savings account.
For each initial amount, work out the amount in the account after

   i 1 year   **ii** 2 years

   a £50 000   **b** £5000   **c** £500   **d** £50

2 Another bank offers 0.5% simple interest on its savings account.
Work out the amount at this bank using the initial amounts in **Q1** parts **a–d** after

   i 1 year   **ii** 2 years

Reflect and reason

What do you notice about your answers to **Q1i** and **Q2ii**? Explain.

⊠ Problem-solving practice

1 When baking, Saul mixes 50 g of sugar with 450 g of flour to make a 500 g mixture.
Chelsea mixes 30 g of sugar with 220 g of flour to make a 250 g mixture.

   a Write the proportion of sugar in Saul's mixture as a percentage.

   b Write the proportion of sugar in Chelsea's mixture as a percentage.

2 Eva and William mix 100 ml of fruit juice with 400 ml of lemonade to make a drink.
Eva and William work out the proportion of the drink that is fruit juice.

Eva writes

$$100 \text{ out of } 400 = \frac{100}{400}$$
$$= \frac{25}{100} = 25\%$$

William writes

$$100 + 400 = 500$$
$$100 \text{ out of } 500 = \frac{100}{500} = \frac{20}{100} = 20\%$$

Who is correct? Explain why.

3 A company that makes batteries claims that 92% of its batteries last for more than 40 hours.

   a Out of 1500 batteries, how many would you expect to last for more than 40 hours?

The company improves its batteries so that the proportion of batteries that last for more than 40 hours increases from 92% to 97%.

   b Out of 1500 batteries, how many would you expect to last for more than 40 hours after the improvement?

4 Sadiq spends £12 000 on a car.
In a year the car decreases in value by 10%.
What is the value of the car after a year?

5 Karl earns £1600 per month.
He then gets a pay rise of 5%.
Work out Karl's monthly pay after his pay rise.

6 A shirt costs £30. It is reduced in a sale by 10%.
Laura says, 'If I buy 2 of the shirts, I will save 20%.'
Laura is incorrect. Explain why.

7 Robert wants to invest £3000.
He considers these two options.
Option A: A savings account for 10 years paying 1.5% simple interest.
Option B: Shares predicted to be worth 12% more in 10 years' time.
Which option is predicted to be worth more? Explain your answer.

Key points

- A multiplier can be used to work out the percentage of an amount. The multiplier is the decimal equivalent of the percentage.
- To increase an amount by a percentage, you can add the percentage to 100%, then work out the multiplier.
- To decrease an amount by a percentage, you can subtract the percentage from 100%, then work out the multiplier.
- Sometimes you want to find the original amount after a percentage increase or decrease. You can use the unitary method.

△ Purposeful practice 1

1 Write the multiplier to work out these percentages of an amount.
   a 80%   **b** 8%   **c** 180%   **d** 108%

2 Write the multiplier to increase an amount by
   a 10%   **b** 11%   **c** 1%   **d** 100%

3 Write the multiplier to decrease an amount by
   a 50%   **b** 55%   **c** 5%   **d** 45%   **e** 95%

Reflect and reason

Renie says, 'The multiplier to increase and decrease an amount by 50% is the same.'
Is Renie correct? Explain.

△ Purposeful practice 2

1 Use a multiplier to increase
   a £70 by 10%   **b** £70 by 20%   **c** £70 by 30%   **d** £70 by 50%
   e 400 g by 10%   **f** 400 g by 20%   **g** 400 g by 30%   **h** 400 g by 50%

2 Use a multiplier to decrease
   a $60 by 10%   **b** $60 by 90%   **c** $60 by 20%   **d** $60 by 80%
   e 200 ml by 10% **f** 200 ml by 90% **g** 200 ml by 20% **h** 200 ml by 80%

Reflect and reason

What do you notice about your answers to **Q2** parts **a** and **b**; parts **c** and **d**; parts **e** and **f**; and parts **g** and **h**?

△ Purposeful practice 3

1 Work out the original distance when
   a 10% of the distance is 300 km   **b** 20% of the distance is 300 km
   c 30% of the distance is 300 km   **d** 40% of the distance is 300 km
   e 80% of the distance is 300 km   **f** 150% of the distance is 300 km

2 Work out the original capacity when

   a 2% of the capacity is 24 litres   **b** 3% of the capacity is 24 litres

   c 6% of the capacity is 24 litres   **d** 8% of the capacity is 24 litres

   e 12% of the capacity is 24 litres   **f** 120% of the capacity is 24 litres

---

Reflect and reason

Jay and Sabina work out **Q1b** differently.

Jay divides by 20 to find 1%, then multiplies by 100 to find 100%.

Sabina notices that 20% × 5 = 100%, so she multiplies by 5 to find 100%.

Which method do you prefer? And do both their methods work when you're given 18% of a distance and asked to find the original? Explain your answer.

⊠ Problem-solving practice

1 Jacob is working out 6% of £92.

He writes

92 × 0.6 = £55.20

Is Jacob correct? Explain why.

2 Match each question in the left-hand box with the correct calculation in the right-hand box.

A:	Increase £120 by 30%
B:	Decrease £120 by 30%
C:	Increase £120 by 70%
D:	Decrease £120 by 70%

E:	120 × 1.3
F:	120 × 1.7
G:	120 × 0.3
H:	120 × 0.7

3 Hannah wants to buy a new bed.

Two shops have the bed in stock but at different prices.

Shop A: £800 plus 20% VAT.

Shop B: £1100 with a discount of 25%.

Which shop should Hannah buy the bed from? Explain why.

4 Cerys has £350 to buy a new phone.

The phone she likes costs £420.

A shop is offering a discount of 15% off all phones.

Does Cerys have enough money to buy the phone from this shop? Explain your answer.

5 Three students are playing a number game.

Manuel says, '20% of my number is 45.'

Marie says, '30% of my number is 45.'

Tessa says, '15% of my number is 45.'

What is the total of all three of their numbers?

6 A TV is reduced by 20% in a sale.

The sale price of the TV is £360.

Work out the original price of the TV.

7 Oliver sells his comic collection.

He makes a profit of 45% compared to its original price.

He sold the comic collection for £174.

How much did the collection originally cost?

Mixed exercises C

Mixed problem-solving practice C

1 Three friends take turns to spin a different spinner each during a game.
The winner is the person who spins the most even numbers.

The probability of Arif's spinner landing on an even number is $\frac{2}{3}$.

The probability of Leon's spinner landing on an even number is $\frac{7}{12}$.

The probability of Ellen's spinner landing on an even number is $\frac{7}{10}$.

Write the friends' names in order, from most likely to win.

2 $\boxed{\frac{2}{3}}$ $\boxed{\frac{7}{8}}$

Which of these fractions has a value closer to $\frac{4}{5}$?
You must show clearly how you get your answer.

3 $\boxed{\frac{3}{4}}$ $\boxed{\frac{1}{5}}$ $\boxed{\frac{1}{2}}$

   a What is the median of these values?

   b Work out the mean of these values.

4 Meg makes paper flowers. She makes 15 flowers each hour.
She makes flowers for $5\frac{1}{2}$ hours each day, on 5 days of the week.
The flowers are packed in boxes. 6 flowers are packed into each box.
How many boxes are needed for all the flowers Meg makes in a week?

5 Jeni grows crops on her farm.
The diagram shows the section of a field where she
grows wheat.
This section of the field growing wheat is 80% of the
whole field.
Work out the area of the whole field.

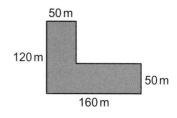

6 A jar contains red, blue and green counters. The number of red counters, the number
of blue counters and the number of green counters are in the ratio 13 : 9 : 18.
Work out what percentage of the counters in the jar are blue.

7 **a** Work out the perimeter of the rectangle.
     Give your answer as a mixed number in inches.

   b Work out the area of the rectangle.
     Give your answer as a mixed number in inches².

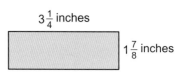

8 $\boxed{\frac{1}{3}}$ $\boxed{\frac{2}{5}}$ $\boxed{\frac{3}{10}}$ $\boxed{\frac{1}{4}}$ $\boxed{\frac{5}{6}}$

Using any two of these fractions for each question part, what is

   a the largest possible total   **b** the smallest possible total
   c the largest possible difference   **d** the smallest possible positive difference
   e the largest possible product   **f** the smallest possible product?

9 Draw the graph of $y = 3x - 1$ for values of x from -2 to 2.

10 A shop sells tea bags in two different-sized boxes.

Box 1: £3.50	Box 2: £5.00
160 tea bags	240 tea bags
Buy 3 boxes and get your fourth box free	15% off price shown

Michelle wants to buy at least 700 tea bags.
What is the cheapest way to do this? Explain why.

11 Mr Ahmed asks 200 students whether they prefer history or geography.
10% of the students prefer history and $\frac{2}{5}$ of the students prefer geography.
The rest of the students do not know.
Two months later, Mr Ahmed asks the same students again.
The number of students who prefer geography has increased by 360%.
The number of students who prefer history has increased by $\frac{1}{10}$.
Work out the number of students who still do not know.

12 An electric company charges customers a fixed
charge per day plus an additional cost for the
amount of electricity, in kilowatt hours, used.
The graph shows information about the total cost
charged.

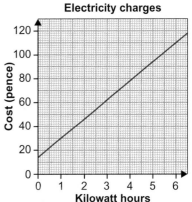

Electricity charges

a What does the y-intercept represent?
b What does the gradient represent?
c Work out the equation of the line.
d Is the cost in direct proportion to how much
electricity is used? Explain how you know.

13 Craig invests £500 at a simple interest rate of 3.5% per year.
At the end of each year, Craig gives the interest to charity.
Work out the least number of years it will take for the total amount he has given to
charity to be greater than £80.

14 The table shows the cost of hiring a tool from a hire company.

Number of days	1	2	3	4
Cost	£30	£35	£40	£45

a Draw a graph to show the cost of hiring the tool.
b Write an equation for the cost of hiring the tool.

15 Khayla is the manager of a shop.
The table gives information about the expenses the shop had last year.

Expense	Wages	Rent	Goods	Other expenses
Amount	£98 000	£12 600	£75 000	£8000

This year:
   the wages will increase by 5%
   the rent will be $\frac{5}{6}$ of the rent last year
   the other expenses will halve
Khayla wants to increase the amount of money she spends on goods.
She also wants the total expenses to be the same as last year.
Can Khayla increase the amount of money she spends on goods?
You must show your working.

Answers

1 Number

1.1 Calculations

Purposeful practice 1

1 a 80   **b** 110   **c** 240   **d** 430   **e** 170   **f** 460
2 a 700   **b** 1300   **c** 2100   **d** 4400   **e** 2600   **f** 3700
3 a 27   **b** 45   **c** 63   **d** 81   **e** 99
4 a 3.3   **b** 5.5   **c** 7.7   **d** 9.9

Purposeful practice 2

1 a 202   **b** 204   **c** 206   **d** 198   **e** 196   **f** 194
2 a 303   **b** 306   **c** 309   **d** 297   **e** 294   **f** 291
3 a 57   **b** 87   **c** 76   **d** 116   **e** 294   **f** 354
4 a 7007   **b** 8008   **c** 6993   **d** 7992   **e** 9009   **f** 8991

Purposeful practice 3

1 a 3895   **b** 3152   **c** 4421   **d** 4210   **e** 6776   **f** 6683
   g 7407   **h** 4824
2 a 28.47   **b** 21.35   **c** 28.1   **d** 22.07   **e** 45.51   **f** 21.11

Problem-solving practice

1 3.5×86 and 7×43; 14×25 and 7×50; 28×25 and 14×50; 14×43 and 7×86; 4.5×86 and 9×43; 18×43 and 9×86
2 By doubling the 50 and halving the 36 to give $100 \times 18 = 1800$
3 22×35 or 5.5×140
4 Cathy is correct because she is the only one to correctly subtract 8 from 8×80. Abi subtracted 79 and Becky added 8.
5 a 7×61 **b** 12×38 **c** 8×97 **d** 11×203
6 2.18 km
7 No, as Jayesh hasn't lined the numbers up correctly, he should have written

```
    5 4 . 3 0
        2 . 8 7
 +  9 6 . 1 0
  1 5 3 . 2 7
        1   1
```

8 1.07 m

1.2 Divisibility

Purposeful practice 1

1 a 42, 428, 504, 672, 846, 1064, 3462
   b 42, 387, 504, 672, 846, 3462
   c 428, 504, 672, 1064
   d 42, 504, 672, 846, 3462
   e 504, 672
2 a Students' own numbers, for example, 18 or 72
   b Students' own numbers, for example, 354 or 624
   c Students' own numbers, for example, 2538 or 9114
3 a Students' own numbers, for example, 48 or 72
   b Students' own numbers, for example, 516 or 924
   c Students' own numbers, for example, 2736 or 3240

Purposeful practice 2

1 a £42.35   **b** £32.65   **c** 52.14   **d** 34.16
2 a 76.8   **b** 824.4   **c** 276.5   **d** 5.45
   e 26.74   **f** 55.65

Problem-solving practice

1 Yes, as the end digit is even so it is divisible by 2,
the digits total 24 which is divisible by 3 so 16 872 is divisible by 3,
the last two digits are 72 which is divisible by 4 so 16 872 is divisible by 4,
16 872 is divisible by 2 and 3 so is divisible by 6 and 16 872 is divisible by 3 and 4 so is divisible by 12.

2 a 1, 4 or 7   **b** 0, 2, 4, 6 or 8
   c 0, 4 or 8   **d** 2 or 8
3 1, 2, 3, 4, 5, 6, 8, 9, 10, 12
4 Students' own 4-digit number that is divisible by 2, 3 and 4, for example, 5784 or 6132.
5

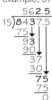

6 a Riya shouldn't have stopped there; she should have added zeros after the 1829.1 and finished the division. She should write each digit of her answer into the correct column to show its value.
   b 152.425

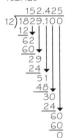

7 £756.25

1.3 Calculating with negative integers

Purposeful practice 1

1 a 6   **b** 5   **c** 4   **d** 3
   e 2   **f** 1   **g** 0   **h** -1
2 a 6   **b** 7   **c** 8   **d** 9
   e 10   **f** 11   **g** 12   **h** 13
3 a E, F   **b** C, D   **c** A, B, G, H

Purposeful practice 2

1 a 20   **b** 20   **c** -20 **d** -20
2 a 8   **b** -8 **c** -8 **d** 8
3 a C, G   **b** A, B, D, E, H   **c** F

Problem-solving practice

1 a No, as Charlie has worked out $-7 - 7$, which is -14, but $-7 - -7 = -7 + 7 = 0$.
   b Yes, when you add -6, you go down 6 and when you subtract 6 you also go down 6.
2 a -9 **b** 2   **c** -32 **d** -9 **e** -7 **f** 19
3 a Students' own answers, for example, $4 - 3$
   b Students' own answers, for example, $1 - 5$
   c Students' own answers, for example, $0 - 10$
   d Students' own answers, for example, $1 + -1$
   e Students' own answers, for example, $-4 + 1$
   f Students' own answers, for example, $-21 + 1$
4 Students' own negative numbers that total -50, for example -20 and -30 (cannot be -25 and -25)
5

6 No, as a negative number multiplied by a negative number is positive so the numbers in the bottom right section have the wrong sign. The grid should be:

×	2	1	0	−1	−2
2	4	2	0	−2	−4
1	2	1	0	−1	−2
0	0	0	0	0	0
−1	−2	−1	0	1	2
−2	−4	−2	0	2	4

7 a −7   **b** −5   **c** 7   **d** −36   **e** 96   **f** 4

8

×	−3	7	−8	11
−2	6	−14	16	−22
−5	15	−35	40	−55
6	−18	42	−48	66
9	−27	63	−72	99

9 −1 × 9, 1 × −9, 3 × −3

1.4 Powers and roots

Purposeful practice 1

1 a 1   **b** 4   **c** 9   **d** 16
  e 25   **f** 36   **g** 49   **h** 64
  i 81   **j** 100   **k** 121   **l** 144
2 a 3 or −3   **b** 6 or −6   **c** 12 or −12   **d** 1 or −1
  e 4 or −4   **f** 10 or −10   **g** 2 or −2   **h** 11 or −11
  i 8 or −8   **j** 5 or −5   **k** 7 or −7   **l** 9 or −9

Purposeful practice 2

1 a 1   **b** −1   **c** 8   **d** −8
  e 27   **f** −27   **g** 64   **h** −64
  i 125   **j** −125   **k** 1000   **l** −1000
2 a 4   **b** 2   **c** 5   **d** 3   **e** 1

Purposeful practice 3

1 12   **2** 32   **3** 4   **4** 2   **5** 12   **6** 32
7 4   **8** 2   **9** 12   **10** 32   **11** −4   **12** $\frac{1}{2}$

Problem-solving practice

1 No, as negative × negative = positive, not negative
2 a 6 or −6   **b** 9 or −9   **c** 12 or −12
  d 9   **e** 49   **f** 100
3 a 14   **b** 4
4 Yes, as $(-6)^3 = -6 \times -6 \times -6 = 36 \times -6 = -216$
5 a 8 or −8   **b** 9 or −9   **c** 10 or −10
  d 1   **e** −1   **f** 5 or −5
6 (0,) 1 and 64
7 A, C and D
8 a 5 cm   **b** 75 cubes   **c** 16 cubes
9 1 (or 0)

1.5 Powers, roots and brackets

Purposeful practice 1

1 a 64   **b** 16   **c** 144   **d** 9
  e 40   **f** 32   **g** 144   **h** 9
2 a 225   **b** 25   **c** 2500   **d** 4
  e 125   **f** 75   **g** 2500   **h** 4

Purposeful practice 2

1 a i 10   **ii** 8   **iii** 4   **iv** 2
  b i 10   **ii** 8   **iii** 4   **iv** 2
2 a i 7   **ii** 6   **iii** 6   **iv** 5
  b i 5.39 (2 d.p.)   **ii** 4.47 (2 d.p.)
    iii 7.75 (2 d.p.)   **iv** 8.66 (2 d.p.)

Purposeful practice 3

1 a 20   **b** 4   **c** 4   **d** 4

2 a 9   **b** 3   **c** 3   **d** 9
3 a 40   **b** 8   **c** 4   **d** 4
4 a 64   **b** 8   **c** 4   **d** 1

Problem-solving practice

1 A, B, C and E
2 $\sqrt{9 + 100}$ because all of the others give an answer of 30.
3 a No, it doesn't give the same answer.
  b It only works if one number is zero.
4 4   **5** $\frac{8^2 + 2^3}{3 - 1} = 36$ **6** $\frac{\sqrt{81} + 3^3}{3^2 \times \sqrt{4}} = 2$

7 No, as Steve has only divided by 4 and not by (4 + 6). Steve should have added 4 and 6 before dividing to give 36 ÷ 10 = 3.6

1.6 More powers, multiples and factors

Purposeful practice 1

1 a 4^5 **b** 5^4 **c** $6^3 \times 7^2$
  d $6^2 \times 7^3$ **e** $3 \times 5^2 \times 7$ **f** $2^3 \times 3 \times 5^2$
2 a 27   **b** 81   **c** 243   **d** 1000   **e** 10 000
  f 100 000   **g** 1   **h** 1   **i** 1   **j** 10

Purposeful practice 2

Students' factor trees may look different, but should have the same prime factors.

1 a
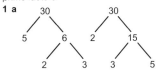

b
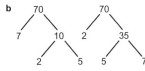

c
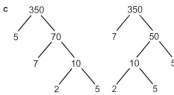

d
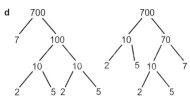

e
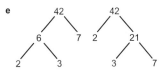

f
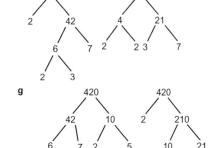

g

h

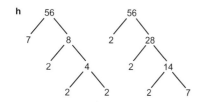

2 a 5×7 **b** $2 \times 5 \times 7$ **c** $2 \times 5 \times 5 \times 7$
  d $2 \times 2 \times 5 \times 5 \times 7$ **e** $2 \times 3 \times 7$ **f** $2 \times 2 \times 3 \times 7$
  g $2 \times 2 \times 3 \times 5 \times 7$ **h** $2 \times 2 \times 2 \times 7$
3 c $2 \times 5^2 \times 7$ **d** $2^2 \times 5^2 \times 7$ **f** $2^2 \times 3 \times 7$
  g $2^2 \times 3 \times 5 \times 7$ **h** $2^3 \times 7$

Purposeful practice 3

1 a 28   **b** 140   **c** 28   **d** 84
2 a 280   **b** 1400   **c** 2100   **d** 2100

Problem-solving practice

1 Lorna should have stopped at the first 5 and circled it as you should never use 1 as it is not a prime number. 9 is 3×3 so she should have factorised 9 into 3 and 3.
2 False. 45 is not a factor of 80.
3 a $60 = 2^2 \times 3 \times 5$ **b** $12 = 2^2 \times 3$
  c Yes, because $12 = 2^2 \times 3$ and $2^2 \times 3$ is also part of the prime factor decomposition of 60
  d Yes, as $648 = 2^3 \times 3^4$ and $36 = 2^2 \times 3^2$
4 $2^3 \times 3^2$
5 No, because the numbers could be 1 and 64, and 2 is not a factor of 1.
6 225   **7** 12
8 120 minutes or 2 hours
9 180

2 Area and volume

2.1 Area of a triangle

Purposeful practice 1

1 a $21\,cm^2$ **b** $24\,cm^2$ **c** $30\,cm^2$
2 a $15\,cm^2$ **b** $18\,cm^2$ **c** $12\,cm^2$
3 a $7.5\,cm^2$ **b** $10\,cm^2$ **c** $12.5\,cm^2$

Purposeful practice 2

1 All three methods give an answer of $14\,cm^2$. Students' own answer to which they find easiest.
2 a Method A: $4.5 \times 2 = 9\,cm^2$
    Method B: $1 \times 9 = 9\,cm^2$
    Method C: $9 \times 2 = 18\,cm^2$, $18 \div 2 = 9\,cm^2$
    Students' own answer to which they find easiest.
  b Method A: $1.5 \times 1.5 = 2.25\,cm^2$
    Method B: $0.75 \times 3 = 2.25\,cm^2$
    Method C: $3 \times 1.5 = 4.5$, $4.5 \div 2 = 2.25\,cm^2$
    Students' own answer to which they find easiest.

Problem-solving practice

1 $26\,cm^2$
2 Sophie is correct as the base of the triangle is 5 and the height is 6, $5 \times 6 = 30$ and half of $30 = 15$. Ruth has incorrectly used $5 + 3 = 8$ as the base. Tristan has used the sloping side of $6.7\,cm$ instead of the perpendicular height.
3 A, C and D all have area of $30\,cm^2$ as 5×12, 10×6 and 15×4 all equal 60.
4 Students' own sketches of two different triangles with an area of $24\,cm^2$, for example triangles with base and height $12\,cm$ and $4\,cm$ or $8\,cm$ and $6\,cm$.
5 $6\,cm$ **6** $360\,cm^2$

2.2 Area of a parallelogram and trapezium

Purposeful practice 1

1 $16\,cm^2$ **2** $20\,cm^2$ **3** $8\,cm^2$
4 $10\,cm^2$ **5** $14\,cm^2$ **6** $12\,cm^2$
7 $6\,cm^2$ **8** $8\,cm^2$ **9** $10\,cm^2$

Purposeful practice 2

1 $15\,cm^2$ **2** $15\,cm^2$ **3** $18\,cm^2$ **4** $21\,cm^2$ **5** $24\,cm^2$
6 $6\,cm^2$ **7** $8\,cm^2$ **8** $18\,cm^2$ **9** $30\,cm^2$ **10** $16.5\,cm^2$

Problem-solving practice

1 Students' own sketches of two different parallelograms with an area of $36\,cm^2$, for example parallelograms with base and height $12\,cm$ and $3\,cm$ or $9\,cm$ and $4\,cm$.
2 Students' own measurements for base and height of a parallelogram that multiply to give an area of $40\,cm^2$, for example $10\,cm$ and $4\,cm$.
3 $64.5\,cm^2$
4 Yes, as area of wall $= \frac{1}{2} \times (1.2 + 2) \times 25 = \frac{1}{2} \times 3.2 \times 25 = 40\,m^2$
5 Yes, Kerry is correct. For each trapezium,
sum of parallel sides $= 16\,cm$ and
perpendicular height $= 4\,cm$, therefore the area of the trapezia will be the same.

2.3 Volume of cubes and cuboids

Purposeful practice 1

1 $1\,cm^3$ **2** $2\,cm^3$ **3** $4\,cm^3$
4 $8\,cm^3$ **5** $12\,cm^3$ **6** $18\,cm^3$
7 $27\,cm^3$ **8** $36\,cm^3$ **9** $48\,cm^3$

Purposeful practice 2

1 $5\,cm^3$ **2** $30\,cm^3$ **3** $35\,cm^3$
4 $28\,cm^3$ **5** $16\,cm^3$ **6** $20\,cm^3$

Problem-solving practice

1 No, as $2 \times 2 \times 2 = 4 \times 2 = 8\,cm^3$; Rory may have added the 2s to work out 2×3 rather than 2^3. Rory has also written the unit as cm^2 but it should be cm^3.
2 Students' own labelled sketches of cuboids with volume $60\,cm^3$, for example with length, width and height of $6\,cm$, $5\,cm$ and $2\,cm$ or $15\,cm$, $2\,cm$ and $2\,cm$.
3 Yes, as the volume of the cube is $3 \times 3 \times 3 = 27\,cm^3$ and $8 \times 27 = 216\,cm^3$.
4 75
5 a $140\,000\,cm^3$ **b** $126\,000\,cm^3$ **c** $8400\,cm^3$
6 $550\,cm^3$

2.4 2D representations of 3D solids

Purposeful practice

1 A and J, B and L, C and G, D and I, E and H, F and K
2 a 2 congruent rectangles, 2 congruent right-angled triangles and 1 more rectangle
  b 2 congruent equilateral triangles, 3 congruent rectangles
  c 2 congruent isosceles triangles, 2 congruent rectangles, 1 other rectangle
  d 4 congruent isosceles triangles, 1 square
3 a Part **c**   **b** Part **d**   **c** Part **b**   **d** Part **a**

Problem-solving practice

1 A, because the four rectangles fold to make the top, bottom and two longer sides and the two squares fold up to make the front and back.
B, because the four rectangles fold to make the top, bottom and two longer sides and the two squares fold up to make the front and back.
D, because the two touching rectangles fold to make the top and a longer side, the two squares fold up to make the front and back and the other two rectangles then fold to make the other longer side and the bottom.
F, because the square attached to the four rectangles is the front and the four rectangles fold to make the top, bottom and two longer sides and the other square folds up to make the back.
2 a Students' own sketch for the net of a cube starting with the 4 squares given, e.g.

b Students should shade two squares on their net that are opposite faces, e.g.

3

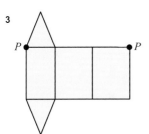

2.5 Surface area of cubes and cuboids

Purposeful practice 1

1 a 6 faces, area $4\,cm \times 4\,cm$
  b $96\,cm^2$
2 a 2 faces, area $4\,cm \times 4\,cm$; 4 faces $4\,cm \times 5\,cm$
  b $112\,cm^2$
3 a 2 faces, area $4\,cm \times 4\,cm$; 4 faces, area $4\,cm \times 6\,cm$
  b $128\,cm^2$
4 a 2 faces, area $5\,cm \times 5\,cm$; 4 faces, area $4\,cm \times 5\,cm$
  b $130\,cm^2$
5 a 2 faces, area $6\,cm \times 5\,cm$; 2 faces, area $5\,cm \times 4\,cm$; 2 faces, area $4\,cm \times 6\,cm$
  b $148\,cm^2$
6 a 2 faces, area $3\,cm \times 5\,cm$; 2 faces, area $5\,cm \times 4\,cm$; 2 faces, area $4\,cm \times 3\,cm$
  b $94\,cm^2$

Purposeful practice 2

1 a $6\,cm^2$ **b** $24\,cm^2$ **c** $600\,cm^2$
2 a i $9\,cm^2$ **ii** $3\,cm$
  b i $25\,cm^2$ **ii** $5\,cm$
  c i $49\,cm^2$ **ii** $7\,cm$
  d i $81\,cm^2$ **ii** $9\,cm$

Problem-solving practice

1 Freya is correct as she has worked out the area of all six faces and added them together. Josh has worked out the volume and Isabel has only worked out the area of the faces she can see so only half of the surface area.
2 a i D   **ii** A   **iii** None   **iv** B   **v** C
  b

3 $4\,cm$
4 Box A, because surface area A $= 14\,300\,cm^2$ and surface area B $= 15\,600\,cm^2$. Students may also add on the inside surface area, in which case these numbers will be doubled.
5 No, as the surface area of one strip is $2 \times 450 \times 20 + 2 \times 20 \times 3 + 2 \times 450 \times 3 = 20\,820\,cm^2$ and of five strips is $20\,820 \times 5 = 104\,100\,cm^2$.
6 The surface area of one cube is $54\,cm^2$ but once two of the faces are glued together, these are not included in the total surface area. So, the surface area for two cubes glued together is $54 \times 2 - 2 \times 9 = 90\,cm^2$ (or $10 \times 9 = 90\,cm^2$).

2.6 Measures

Purposeful practice 1

1 a i $30\,mm$ and $50\,mm$ **ii** $1500\,mm^2$
  b i $50\,mm$ and $20\,mm$ **ii** $1000\,mm^2$
  c i $300\,mm$ and $200\,mm$ **ii** $60\,000\,mm^2$
2 a i $15\,cm^2$ **ii** $1500\,mm^2$
  b i $10\,cm^2$ **ii** $1000\,mm^2$
  c i $600\,cm^2$ **ii** $60\,000\,mm^2$
3 a i $2\,cm$ and $2.5\,cm$ **ii** $5\,cm^2$
  b i $2\,cm$ and $4.5\,cm$ **ii** $9\,cm^2$
  c i $75\,cm$ and $20\,cm$ **ii** $1500\,cm^2$

4 a i $500\,mm^2$ **ii** $5\,cm^2$
  b i $900\,mm^2$ **ii** $9\,cm^2$
  c i $150\,000\,mm^2$ **ii** $1500\,cm^2$

Purposeful practice 2

1 a i $300\,cm$ and $200\,cm$ **ii** $60\,000\,cm^2$
  b i $50\,cm$ and $40\,cm$ **ii** $2000\,cm^2$
  c i $4000\,cm$ and $1200\,cm$ **ii** $4\,800\,000\,cm^2$
2 a i $6\,m^2$ **ii** $60\,000\,cm^2$
  b i $0.2\,m^2$ **ii** $2000\,cm^2$
  c i $480\,m^2$ **ii** $4\,800\,000\,cm^2$

Problem-solving practice

1 Lexi and Sanjay are correct as Lexi has correctly worked out the area in cm^2 and has then correctly converted it to mm^2. Sanjay has converted the lengths to mm first and then correctly worked out the area. Isaac has correctly worked out the area in cm^2 but then has converted it to mm^2 incorrectly because he used $1\,cm = 10\,mm$ which is the conversion for length, not area.
2 Area of parallelogram $= 200 \times 72 = 14\,400\,mm^2$, area of rectangle $= 24 \times 6 = 144\,cm^2 = 14\,400\,mm^2$, so both areas are the same.
  Students may also calculate both areas as $144\,cm^2$.
3 a $3\,cm^2$ **b** $150\,000\,cm^2$ **c** $2500\,cm^2$
  d $0.96\,cm^2$ **e** $150\,000\,cm^2$
4 $0.576\,m^2$
5 $140\,cm$
6 Students' own sketch of a rectangle with area $72\,cm^2$, e.g. a rectangle with length and width $120\,mm$ and $60\,mm$.
7 A has the largest area because the areas are A: $5000\,cm^2$, B: $4200\,cm^2$, C: $4000\,cm^2$, D: $4675\,cm^2$ and E: $4900\,cm^2$.

3 Statistics, graphs and charts

3.1 Pie charts

Purposeful practice 1

1 b $\frac{1}{4}$, 50 students   **c** $\frac{1}{4}$, 50 students
2 Maths $\frac{1}{4}$, 40 students. Art $\frac{1}{8}$, 20 students. Science $\frac{1}{8}$, 20 students. English $\frac{1}{2}$, 80 students.
3 a i 60   **ii** 30   **iii** 30   **b** 240
4 a i 45   **ii** 90   **b** 180

Purposeful practice 2

1

Percentage of data	Angle
100%	360°
50%	**180°**
25%	90°
10%	**36°**
20%	72°

2 Black 144°, brown 72°, blonde 90°, red 36°, grey 18°

Problem-solving practice

1 288
2 210
3 a James hasn't worked out the angles. He has used the percentages as the angles which means there is space in the pie chart he has not used.
  b A labelled pie chart with angles 144°, 108°, 72° and 36°

3.2 Using tables

Purposeful practice 1

1 1.22   **2** 1   **3** 3.2

Purposeful practice 2

1

Length	Tally	Frequency
$0 \leq l < 3$	I	1
$3 \leq l < 6$	℻	5
$6 \leq l < 9$	III	3
$9 \leq l < 12$	III	3
$12 \leq l < 15$	II	2

2

Length	Tally	Frequency
$2 \leq l < 5$	IIII	4
$5 \leq l < 8$	IIII	4
$8 \leq l < 11$	III	3
$11 \leq l < 14$	III	3

Problem-solving practice

1 a Emma has divided by 5 instead of the total frequency, which is 20.

  b Ben has only divided the 8 by 20, instead of dividing the total 31 by 20.

  c 1.55

2 a 26.35 g

  b The mean will decrease as 25 g is less than the mean of 26.35 g.

3 No, as the mean is 34.96.

3.3 Stem and leaf diagrams

Purposeful practice 1

	a	b	c
1	3	2	7
2	5	3	9
3	7	4	10
4	4	2.5	7
5	4	2.5	8
6	4	2.5	9
7	6	3.5	9
8	6	3.5	9.5
9	6	3.5	10.5

Purposeful practice 2

	a	b	c	d	e	f
1	23	2.3	£2.33	57	5.7	43
2	26	2.6	£2.45	26	2.6	26
3	23	2.3	£2.33	57	5.7	54

Problem-solving practice

1 No, as $\frac{10 + 1}{2} = 5.5$, so the median will be the number halfway between the 5th and 6th cards.

2 15

3 a 25

  b Students' own answers; any number from 1 to 19 apart from 6.

4 a The full list of numbers is **15**, 19, **22**, **22**, 24, 25, **27**, **27**, **27**, 30, 32, **32**, **35**, 37, 38, **41**, 45, 50, 52, **55**.

```
1 | 5 9
2 | 2 2 4 5 7 7 7
3 | 0 2 2 5 7 8
4 | 1 5
5 | 0 2 5
Key: 1|5 means 15
```

  b Mode = 27, median = 31, range = 40

5 a 21   **b** 9   **c** 56 mm   **d** 57 mm   **e** 44 mm

  f Yes, as median = 111 mm and 111 − 57 = 54 mm which is over 50 mm.
Students could also use the mean value of 108 mm to justify their answer.

3.4 Comparing data

Purposeful practice 1

1 A 0, B 1, C 2, D 4, E 9   **2** A   **3** E

Purposeful practice 2

1 a A 6, B 4.75, C 5.75, D 6.25, E 4.5

  b D   **c** E

2 a, b

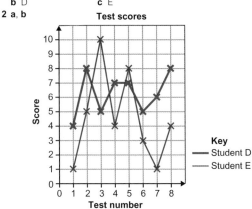

c No, in tests 3 and 5, D scored lower than E, even though D has a higher mean score.

3 a

Test scores graph

b No, score for C is equal to score for B in test 5 and test 8. Score for C is higher in all other tests.

Problem-solving practice

1 a Rajiv as his range is 4, which is lower than Andy's range of 7.

  b Andy as his mean is 9, which is higher than Rajiv's mean of 8.

2 a A 30°C, B 33°C   **b** A 1 mm, B 67 mm

  c A 3°C, B 2°C   **d** A 5 mm, B 125 mm

  e Students' own answer with reasons given using mean and range. For example, destination A because although the mean temperature is slightly lower than the mean for destination B, the mean rainfall is much lower and more consistent for destination A compared to destination B.

3 Christchurch was warmer as its mean temperature was 16.8°C (1 d.p.) and London's mean temperature was 15.6°C (1 d.p.).

3.5 Scatter graphs

Purposeful practice 1

1 a

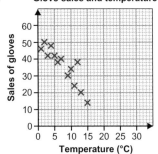

Glove sales and temperature

b Negative

c As temperature increases, gloves sales decrease.

2 a

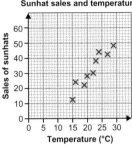

Sunhat sales and temperature

b Positive

c As temperature increases, sunhat sales increase.

3 a

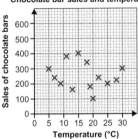

Chocolate bar sales and temperature

b No correlation

c No, there is no clear relationship between the temperature and the number of chocolate bars sold.

Purposeful practice 2

1 a A **b** C **c** F

2

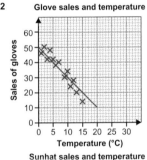

Glove sales and temperature

Sunhat sales and temperature

Problem-solving practice

1 a and **b** Students' line of best fit, e.g.:

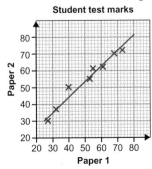

Student test marks

c Positive correlation

2 a Negative correlation   **b** None

  c Negative correlation   **d** Positive correlation

3 a None; there is no relationship between house prices and students' arrival times for school.

b Positive correlation; higher amounts spent on advertising a toy are likely to result in higher sales.

c Negative correlation; the value of a car is likely to decrease with age.

d Positive correlation; increased rainfall is likely to lead to higher umbrella sales.

e None; no relationship between student height and performance in maths exams.

f Positive correlation; it is likely that taller people will have a greater arm span.

3.6 Misleading graphs

Purposeful practice

1 a **i** 3   **ii** More information needed

     iii More information needed   **iv** No

      v More information needed   **vi** More information needed

  b **iii** 17–25   **v** Blue, red and grey

  c **ii** 36   **vi** 160

2 a

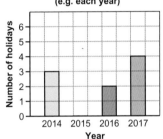

Number of holidays (e.g. each year)

b

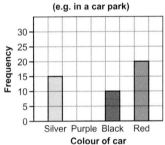

Colours of car (e.g. in a car park)

Problem-solving practice

1 a Games console   **b** Playing sport

  c 24   **d** 20

  e No, as for school A it is 30% of 120 = 36 and for school B it is 25% of 200 = 50, so even though the sector/percentage is smaller it represents, more students.

2 No, as 870 is not double 730. The vertical axis does not start from 0.

Mixed problem-solving practice A

1 £359.25

2 No, as $-1 \times -7 = 7$, not -7. Fay should have said her number is 7 times Suha's number.

3 No, $5^2 = 25$ and $(-5)^2 = 25$, so $5^2 = (-5)^2$ is correct but $5^3 = 125$ and $(-5)^3 = -125$, so $5^3 = (-5)^3$ is not correct.

4 Yes, as the area of the triangle = $24\,\text{cm}^2$ and the area of the parallelogram = $144\,\text{cm}^2$ and $6 \times 24 = 144$.

5 $9\,\text{cm}^2$

6 a

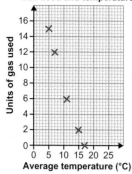

Gas used and temperature

Units of gas used vs Average temperature (°C)

b Negative correlation. The higher the average temperature is, the fewer units of gas are used to heat the house.

c

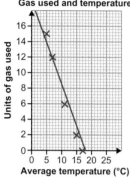

Gas used and temperature

Units of gas used vs Average temperature (°C)

7 a Students' own net of the cuboid, for example

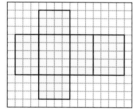

b $60\,cm^3$ **c** $94\,cm^2$

8 £47.97

9 150

10 a

14	9
15	4 5
16	1 3 5 5 9
17	1 4 5 8

Key: 14 | 9 means 149 cm

b Year 7 median = 165 cm and range = 29 cm
Year 8 median = 171 cm and range = 23 cm
So on average, the Year 8 students are taller and their heights are more consistent than the heights of the Year 7 students.

11 a Pie chart divided into following sectors:
Photography 168°
Business studies 120°
Tourism 72°

Year 8 subject choices

Photography, Business studies, Tourism

b No, as we don't know how many students are in Year 9.

12 9.15 am

13 $729\,cm^3$

14 a 0   **b** 5.9

4 Expressions and equations

4.1 Algebraic powers

Purposeful practice 1

1 a x^2 **b** x^3 **c** x^4 **d** x^5
 e t^5 **f** t^3 **g** t^4 **h** t^2

2 a $m \times m \times m \times m$ **b** $m \times m \times m \times m \times m$
 c $y \times y \times y$ **d** $y \times y \times y \times y \times y \times y$
 e $y \times y$

3 b $3x$ **c** $4x$ **d** $5x$ **e** $5t$
 f $3t$ **g** $4t$ **h** $2t$

4 b $y + y + y + y + y + y$ **c** $y + y$
 d $m + m + m + m$ **e** $m + m + m + m + m$

5 b $6 \times y$ **c** $2 \times y$ **d** $4 \times m$ **e** $5 \times m$

Purposeful practice 2

1 $2^2 \times 3$ **2** 2×3^2 **3** $3^2 \times 5$
4 $r^2 s$ **5** rs^2 **6** $s^2 t$
7 $2^2 \times 3^2$ **8** $2^2 \times 5^2$ **9** $2^2 \times 5^3$
10 $r^2 s^2$ **11** $r^2 t^2$ **12** $r^2 t^3$
13 $2^2 \times 3^3$ **14** $3^2 \times 5^2$ **15** $5^2 \times 2^3$
16 $r^2 s^3$ **17** $s^2 t^2$ **18** $r^3 t^2$

Problem-solving practice

1 Ian is not correct. $y \times y \times y = y^3$ not $3y$
2 a $4s$ **b** $6h$
3 $x \times x \times x \times x \times x$ because $x + x + x + x + x = 5x$ and 5^x is 5 multiplied by itself x times, not x multiplied by itself 5 times.
4 $5 \times 5 \times 5 \times 7 \times 7 \times 7$
5 Jamal has only squared the b, not the a.
$a \times a \times b \times b = a^2 b^2$
6 A and I, B and L, C and J, D and G, E and H, F and K
7 a $a \times a \times b \times b \times b$
 b $a \times b \times b \times b \times b$
8

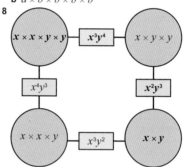

4.2 Expressions and brackets

Purposeful practice 1

1 a $2t + 6$ **b** $-2t - 6$ **c** $2t - 6$
 d $-2t + 6$ **e** $6 + 2t$ **f** $-6 - 2t$
 g $-6 + 2t$ **h** $6 - 2t$ **i** $6 - 2t$
 j $-6 + 2t$ **k** $-6 - 2t$ **l** $6 + 2t$
 m $10t + 6$ **n** $-10t - 6$ **o** $10t - 6$
 p $-10t + 6$ **q** $10t^2 + 6t$ **r** $-10t^2 - 6t$
 s $10t^2 - 6t$ **t** $-10t^2 + 6t$

2 a $5x + 12$ **b** $12x + 5$ **c** $12x - 5$
 d $5x + 2$ **e** $5x - 12$ **f** $-2x - 5$
 g $5 - 5x$ **h** $15 - 5x$ **i** $5x - 5$
 j $5x + 5$ **k** $-2 - 5x$ **l** $8 - 5x$

Purposeful practice 2

1 a a **b** $-a$ **c** -4 **d** -4
 e $-4a$ **f** $-4a$ **g** a **h** 4
2 a $-x - 2$ **b** $-x + 2$ **c** $-2x - 1$ **d** $-2x + 1$
3 a $3 - x$ **b** $7 - x$ **c** $4x + 2$ **d** $4x - 2$
 e $4x - 1$ **f** $4x - 5$
4 a $7 + x$ **b** $3 + x$ **c** $6x + 2$ **d** $6x - 2$
 e $6x + 3$ **f** $6x - 5$

Problem-solving practice

1 a Rectangle D
  b Rectangle A
  c Rectangle C
  d Rectangle B

2 a $-3(a - 2) = -3a + 6$ **b** $-2(-5b - 7) = 10b + 14$

3 $2(2x - 4), -2(-2x + 4), 4(x - 2), -4(-x + 2), -(-4x + 8)$

4

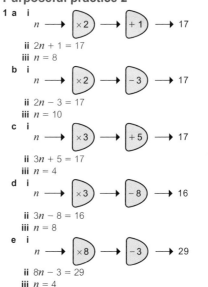

5 $5m$

6 $2(x - 3) + 7$ and $2x + 1$, $2(x - 4) + 7$ and $2x - 1$,
$7 - (-2x + 3)$ and $2x + 4$, $7 + (-2x + 4)$ and $-2x + 11$,
$7 - (2x + 3)$ and $-2x + 4$, $7 - (-2x - 3)$ and $2x + 10$

7 a Alice has worked out $-5 - 3$, not $-5 + 3$.
  b Helen has expanded the brackets incorrectly: she has not multiplied the -3 by -1.
  c $3x - 2$

4.3 Factorising expressions

Purposeful practice 1

1 a $3(x + 3)$ **b** $3(x + 2)$ **c** $3(x + 1)$
2 a $5(a + 1)$ **b** $5(a + 2)$ **c** $5(a + 3)$
3 a $4(m - 3)$ **b** $4(m - 2)$ **c** $4(m - 1)$
4 a $7(y - 1)$ **b** $7(y - 2)$ **c** $7(y - 3)$

Purposeful practice 2

1 a $3(2x + 3)$ **b** $3(2x + 5)$ **c** $3(2x + 7)$
2 a $2(2a - 3)$ **b** $2(2a - 5)$ **c** $2(2a - 7)$
3 a $5(3n + 2)$ **b** $5(5n + 2)$ **c** $5(7n + 2)$
4 a $2(4h - 3)$ **b** $2(4h - 5)$ **c** $2(4h - 7)$
5 a $4(2t + 3)$ **b** $4(2t + 5)$ **c** $4(2t + 7)$
6 a $10(2y - 3)$ **b** $10(2y - 5)$ **c** $10(2y - 7)$
7 a $a(a + 1)$ **b** $a(a - 1)$ **c** $a(2a - 1)$
  d $b(2b + 1)$ **e** $b(2b + 3)$ **f** $b(3b - 2)$
  g $b(5b - 2)$ **h** $b(5b - 3)$ **i** $b(5b + 3)$
8 a $2c(c + 3)$ **b** $2c(c + 2)$ **c** $2c(c + 1)$
9 a $3d(d + 3)$ **b** $3d(d + 2)$ **c** $3d(d + 1)$
10 a $3e(2e + 3)$ **b** $3e(2e + 5)$ **c** $2f(2f - 3)$
  d $2f(2f + 7)$ **e** $4g(2 - 3g)$ **f** $4g(2 - 5g)$
  g $4g(2g - 5)$ **h** $10x(2x - 3)$ **i** $10x(2 - 5x)$

Problem-solving practice

1 a Karen
  b Kris has subtracted the 4 from the 12 and 16 instead of dividing them by 4. Harry has not divided the 16 by 4.

2 $60t^2 - 25t$ and $5t(12t - 5)$, $60t^2 - 14t$ and $2t(30t - 7)$,
$60t^2 - 50t$ and $10t(6t - 5)$, $60t^2 - 48t$ and $12t(5t - 4)$,
$60t^2 - 16t$ and $4t(15t - 4)$, $60t^2 - 42t$ and $6t(10t - 7)$

3 The HCF is $9a$, not 3, and there should be '$-$' in the brackets, not '$+$'. The correct answer is $9a(2a - 3)$.

4 a $10a - 35 = 5(2a - 7)$
  b $6b^2 + 14b = 2b(3b + 7)$

5 Yes, Samar is correct as $20y - 28 = 4(5y - 7)$ and
$35y^2 - 49y = 7y(5y - 7)$. $(5y - 7)$ is a factor of both expressions.

6 a Rectangle C   **b** Rectangle D
  c Rectangle A   **d** Rectangle B

7 a 7 and $(4h^2 - 5h)$ or $7h$ and $(4h - 5)$ or h and $(28h - 35)$
  b 7 and $(4h^2 - 5h)$ or $7h$ and $(4h - 5)$ or h and $(28h - 35)$, depending on answer to part **a**
  c $7h$ and $(4h - 5)$

8 a Yes, because addition is commutative.
  b No, because subtraction is not commutative.

4.4 One-step equations

Purposeful practice 1

1 a $x = 0$ **b** $x = -1$ **c** $x = -2$
  d $x = -7$ **e** $y = 7$ **f** $y = 6$
  g $y = 5$ **h** $y = 3$ **i** $z = -5$
  j $z = 55$ **k** $z = 5$ **l** $z = -3$
  m $n = 5$ **n** $p = -25$

Purposeful practice 2

1 a $x = 3$ **b** $x = 9$ **c** $x = 35$
  d $x = 0$ **e** $x = 1$ **f** $x = 5$
  g $x = 0$ **h** $x = 2$ **i** $x = 20$
  j $x = 15$ **k** $x = 12$ **l** $x = 10$
  m $x = 6$ **n** $x = 5$ **o** $x = 4$
2 a $n = 12$ **b** $n = 4$ **c** $n = 6$
  d $n = 18$ **e** $n = 6$ **f** $n = 9$
  g $n = 48$ **h** $n = 36$ **i** $n = 60$
  j $n = 100$ **k** $n = 200$ **l** $n = 300$
3 a $r = 3$ **b** $r = 48$ **c** $t = 8$
  d $t = 32$ **e** $m = 150$ **f** $m = 6$
4 a $y = -1$ **b** $y = -2$ **c** $y = -5$
  d $y = -1$ **e** $y = -2$ **f** $y = -5$
  g $y = 1$ **h** $y = 2$ **i** $y = 5$

Problem-solving practice

1 Victor reversed the function machine but he didn't use the inverse function of '$+6$' to give an answer of $y = 16$.

2 A and C $(x = 7)$, B, E and H $(x = 8)$, D, F and G $(x = 9)$

3 a $6n = 36$ **b** $n = 6$
4 a $5x = 60$ **b** $x = 12$
5 a $4s = 36$ **b** $s = 9$
6 a $12a = 360$ **b** $a = 30$
7 a $10x = 60$ **b** $x = 6$

4.5 Two-step equations

Purposeful practice 1

1 a $x = 6$ **b** $n = 9$ **c** $a = 10$
  d $b = 5$ **e** $c = 10$ **f** $d = -5$
2 a $e = 2$ **b** $f = -2$ **c** $g = 4$
  d $h = 4$ **e** $k = 1$ **f** $m = -1$
3 a $n = 5$ **b** $p = 7$ **c** $q = 7$
  d $r = 13$ **e** $s = 10$ **f** $t = 30$
  g $u = -10$ **h** $v = 30$

Purposeful practice 2

1 a i $n \longrightarrow \boxed{\times 2} \longrightarrow \boxed{+ 1} \longrightarrow 17$
  ii $2n + 1 = 17$
  iii $n = 8$
b i $n \longrightarrow \boxed{\times 2} \longrightarrow \boxed{- 3} \longrightarrow 17$
  ii $2n - 3 = 17$
  iii $n = 10$
c i $n \longrightarrow \boxed{\times 3} \longrightarrow \boxed{+ 5} \longrightarrow 17$
  ii $3n + 5 = 17$
  iii $n = 4$
d i $n \longrightarrow \boxed{\times 3} \longrightarrow \boxed{- 8} \longrightarrow 16$
  ii $3n - 8 = 16$
  iii $n = 8$
e i $n \longrightarrow \boxed{\times 8} \longrightarrow \boxed{- 3} \longrightarrow 29$
  ii $8n - 3 = 29$
  iii $n = 4$

2 a $5x + 3$ **b** $5x + 3 = 13$ **c** £2

Problem-solving practice

1 Amir has used the correct inverse for each function but has changed their order. The ÷2 and +8 need swapping over. The correct answer is $x = 15$.

2 a $6n - 5 = 67$ **b** 12

3 a $5a + 55 = 180$ **b** $a = 25$

4 a $4x + 5 = 21$ **b** $x = 4$

5 a $4t + 12 = 28$ **b** $t = 4$

6 a i–viii All answers are $y = 50$

  b All answers are the same. Using a function machine, each equation results in $50 \div 5$ as the numbers total 50 in each question ($26 + 24 = 50$, etc.).

  c No, this is not the case, because the numbers add up to 50 but you then need to divide by 10.

7 a $2x + 75 = 81$ ($x = 3$)

  b $2x - 75 = 81$ ($x = 78$)

8 $3P + 25 = 94$, so $P = £23$

4.6 The balancing method

Purposeful practice 1

1 a $x = 5$ **b** $y = 19$ **c** $z = 19$

  d $a = -5$ **e** $b = -19$ **f** $c = 5$

2 a $d = 3$ **b** $e = -3$ **c** $f = 3$ **d** $g = -3$

  e $h = 30$ **f** $i = -30$ **g** $j = -30$ **h** $k = 30$

3 a $m = 20$ **b** $n = -20$ **c** $r = 10$

  d $s = -10$ **e** $t = -10$ **f** $u = 10$

4 a $v = 8$ **b** $w = 11$ **c** $x = 6$

  d $y = 5$ **e** $z = -1$ **f** $a = -1$

5 a $b = -4$ **b** $c = -3$ **c** $d = -2$

  d $e = 2$ **e** $f = 3$ **f** $g = -4$

Purposeful practice 2

1 a $P = 28$ **b** $s = 3$

2 a $A = 35$ **b** $l = 4$ **c** $w = 3$

3 a $A = 48$ **b** $b = 4$ **c** $h = 10$

4 a $A = 15$ **b** $h = 4$ **c** $b = 9$

5 a £160   **b** $d = 5$

Problem-solving practice

1 a $y = 47$ **b** $x = 12$

2 $l = 13$

3 $l = 12\,\text{cm}$

4 a $x = 4.5$ **b** $9\,\text{cm}$

5 $x = 54°$

6 Sara has added 2 instead of dividing by -2 to give $x = -4$.

5 Real-life graphs

5.1 Conversion graphs

Purposeful practice 1

1 a 22 lb   **b** 15 kg

2 a 11 lb   **b** 2.2 lb   **c** 30 kg   **d** 0.45 kg

Purposeful practice 2

1 a

Centimetre	0	1	5
Millimetre	0	10	50

b i 5   **ii** 50

c, d

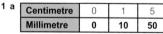
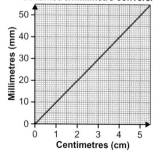

Centimetre/millimetre conversion

---

2 a

Miles	0	5	10
Kilometres	0	8	16

b i 10   **ii** 16

c, d

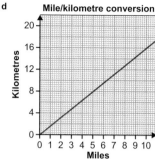

Mile/kilometre conversion

Problem-solving practice

1 Harrison, as 2 litres ≈ 3.5 pints or 3 pints ≈ 1.7 litres.

2 £62.50 (or a similar answer with valid working).

An example of working is: using the graph, €30 ≈ £25 and €15 ≈ £12.50, so €75 = 25 + 25 + 12.50 = £62.50.

3

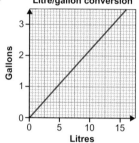

Litre/gallon conversion

4

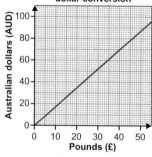

Pound/Australian dollar conversion

5 a

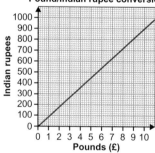

Pound/Indian rupee conversion

  b £2.93 (answers may vary slightly from reading the graph).

6 Dean; Students' own graph showing that 1 gallon corresponds to about 4.5 litres.

5.2 Distance–time graphs

Purposeful practice 1

	Journey 1	Journey 2	Journey 3
A: Distance travelled	40 miles	50 km	10 km
A: Time spent travelling	1 hour	$\frac{1}{2}$ hour (30 minutes)	2 hours
B: Time spent not moving	$\frac{1}{2}$ hour (30 minutes)	$\frac{1}{4}$ hour (15 minutes)	1 hour
C: Distance travelled	50 miles	75 km	15 km
C: Time spent travelling	$1\frac{1}{2}$ hours (90 minutes)	$\frac{3}{4}$ hours (45 minutes)	3 hours
Total distance travelled	90 miles	125 km	25 km
Total time	3 hours	$1\frac{1}{2}$ hours	6 hours

Purposeful practice 2

1 a A: 80 km/h, B: 60 km/h, C: 90 km/h
  b Car C

2 a

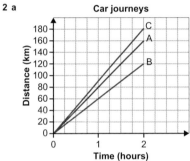

Car journeys

  b Car C

Problem-solving practice

1 No, Levi cycled faster on the way to Derby as the lines for his movement are steeper than those for Cameron. They both cycled home at the same speed as the lines are parallel.

2 a

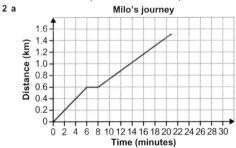

Milo's journey

  b 2 minutes   **c** 0.9 km

3

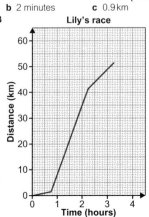

Lily's race

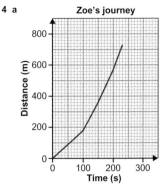

Zoe's journey

  b Faster, as each section of the graph is steeper than the previous one.

5.3 Line graphs

Purposeful practice 1

1 There were 20 ice cream vans in operation, the average daily temperature was 25 °C, and there were 8000 tourists.

2 From left to right: 6 vans, 22.2 °C, 2400 tourists

3

Month	May	Jun	Jul	Aug	Sep	Oct
Number of ice cream vans in operation	6	10	17	20	13	5

Month	May	Jun	Jul	Aug	Sep	Oct
Average daily temperature (°C)	22.2	23.0	24.4	25.0	23.6	22.0

Month	May	Jun	Jul	Aug	Sep	Oct
Number of tourists	2400	4000	6800	8000	5200	2000

4 From left to right: 15 vans, 3.0 °C, 6000 tourists
5 May to August
6 August to October

Purposeful practice 2

1

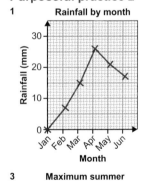

Rainfall by month

2

Sales

3

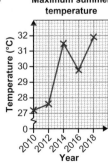

Maximum summer temperature

Problem-solving practice

1 a 14°C   **b** 9°C
  c No, as there is a slight decrease from April to May and from September to October it stays the same.

2 a June   **b** 66

3 The vertical axis 'Average rainfall (m)' is not labelled.
The gap between 2017 and 2018 is bigger than the other years (they should all be the same).
Only the point for 2014 at 1.5 is plotted correctly; the others are all incorrect.

5.4 More line graphs

Purposeful practice 1

b i	2.3 million	**ii**	2 300 000
c i	0.3 million	**ii**	300 000
d i	1.6 million	**ii**	1 600 000
e i	4.2 million	**ii**	4 200 000
f i	0.4 million	**ii**	400 000
g i	1.6 million	**ii**	1 600 000
h i	4.8 million	**ii**	4 800 000
i i	9.6 million	**ii**	9 600 000
j i	46 million	**ii**	46 000 000
k i	24 million	**ii**	24 000 000
l i	8 million	**ii**	18 000 000

Purposeful practice 2

1

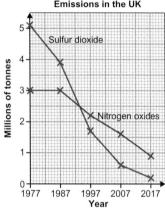

2 Emissions of both sulfur dioxide and nitrogen oxides have decreased/are decreasing.

3 1993/4 – the graph lines cross.

4 Sulfur dioxide – the trend or line is steeper.

Problem-solving practice

1 No, as the population in 1951 and 2011 is 8.2 million and in 1981 it is 6.7 million. Half of 8.2 million is 4.1 million, not 6.7 million.

2 a The trend of the TV viewing figures for programme A is increasing. The trend of the TV viewing figures for programme B is decreasing.
  b i 3.6 million   **ii** 1.1 million

3 a

  b The trend for both shops is increasing sales.
  c £0.7 million   **d** £0.1 million

5.5 Real-life graphs

Purposeful practice 1

1 The trend is that her marks are increasing.

2 4

3 Yes, because her marks have been above the pass mark for 4 weeks, and are increasing.

Purposeful practice 2

1 55%

2 Decreasing (more slowly since around 1995).

3 Increasing (more slowly since around 1998).

Problem-solving practice

1 a Students' scales may differ

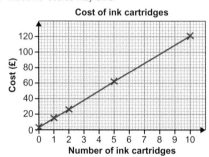

  b £3

2 a No, the trend is that the percentage profit for the company is increasing.
  b Cannot know, because the graph is showing the profit as percentages, not the actual profit.
  c Company B because it has stayed at a similar level (between 50% and 56%) from 2015 to 2018.

3 a A: company X, B: company Z and C: company Y
  b £12
  c No, line B for company Z is steeper than line A for company X so they will cross, meaning company Z will then become more expensive.

5.6 Curved graphs

Purposeful practice

1 a i Sample A   **ii** Sample B
  b 15 seconds   **c** 30 seconds
  d Sample A   **e** Sample A

2 a

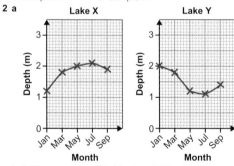

  b 2.05 m   **c** January to March   **d** March to May

Problem-solving practice

1 a Sulfur, as it is an upward curve.
  b Calcium carbonate, as it is a downward curve.
  c No, as the curve for sulfur is steeper than the curve for calcium carbonate.

2 P: D and H
  Q: C and J
  R: E and F
  S: A and I
  T: B and G

3 a Priya by 16 seconds, as Priya finishes at 92 s and Deana at 108 s.
  b No, as Priya's curve is not steeper than Deana's for the whole race.

6 Decimals and ratio

6.1 Ordering decimals and rounding

Purposeful practice 1

1 a i 905.6   **ii** 905.63   **iii** 905.632
   b i 90.6   **ii** 90.56   **iii** 90.563
   c i 9.1   **ii** 9.06   **iii** 9.056
   d i 0.9   **ii** 0.91   **iii** 0.906
   e i 0.1   **ii** 0.09   **iii** 0.091

2 a i 8.4   **ii** 8
   b i 0.8   **ii** 0.8
   c i 0.1   **ii** 0.08
   d i 0.0   **ii** 0.008

3 a i 40.04   **ii** 40
   b i 4.00   **ii** 4.0
   c i 0.40   **ii** 0.40
   d i 0.04   **ii** 0.040

4 a i £2.49   **ii** £2.49
   b i £24.94   **ii** £24.90
   c i £249.37   **ii** £249.00
   d i £2493.72   **ii** £2490.00
   e i £24 937.16   **ii** £24 900.00
   f i £249 371.63   **ii** £249 000.00

Purposeful practice 2

1 a <   **b** >   **c** >   **d** >   **e** <   **f** <   **g** >
2 a 29.6061, 29.6, 29.0601, 29.0061
   b 9.216, 9.201 06, 9.200 16, 9.020 16
   c −3.247, −3.4, −3.724, −4.32
   d 0.308, 0.083, −0.803, −0.83

Problem-solving practice

1 a Any number from 4.55 to 4.6
   b Any number from 4.6 to 4.649 99...
2 B, C and D
3 Students' own answers, e.g. 1.234 < 1.324.
4 Yes, because the whole number parts are the same but when comparing the tenths, 4 is greater than 3.
5 6.9 as it should be last in the list because 9 is greater than 8.
6 When comparing the tenths, they are both 2; when comparing the hundredths, 0 is less than 3.
7 Any three numbers from 6.735 to 6.744 99...
8 Students' own answer that rounds to 4.23 to 2 d.p. and 4.230 to 3 d.p., so any one of: 4.2300, 4.2301, 4.2302 or 4.2304.
9 Any number from 12.701 to 12.719.
10 a Any number using the digits allowed where the hundredths digit is 9.
   b Any number using the digits allowed where the hundredths digit is 9.
11 a–d round down because the numbers in the thousandths column are 1–4. **e–i** round up because the numbers in the thousandths column are 5–9.
12 a £333.33
   b No, as £333.33 × 3 = £999.99, so she has 1p left that can't be distributed evenly.

6.2 Place-value calculations

Purposeful practice 1

1 a 1263   **b** 9683   **c** 51 783   **d** 1448   **e** 12 308
   f 120 908   **g** 5250   **h** 14 000   **i** 189 000
2 a 27 459   **b** 136 764   **c** 353 306   **d** 749 504

Purposeful practice 2

1 a 516   **b** 51.6   **c** 5.16   **d** 0.516
   e 918   **f** 91.8   **g** 9.18   **h** 0.918
2 a 14 145   **b** 1414.5   **c** 141.45   **d** 141.45
   e 14.145   **f** 14.145
3 a 20 592   **b** 2059.2   **c** 205.92   **d** 205.92
   e 20.592   **f** 20.592
4 a 181 308   **b** 18 130.8   **c** 1813.08   **d** 181.308
   e 18 130.8   **f** 1813.08   **g** 181.308   **h** 1813.08

Purposeful practice 3

1 6   **2** 0.6   **3** 0.06   **4** 49
5 4.9   **6** 0.49   **7** 173   **8** 17.3
9 1.73   **10** 52.8   **11** 5.28   **12** 0.528

Problem-solving practice

1 a He has multiplied 237 by 6 and then 4 instead of by 6 and then 40.
   b 10 902   **c** 109.02
2 Grace has put the decimal point in the wrong place: it should be 18.424.
3 Yes, as you work out 235 × 87 first and then divide the answer by 100 to give the answer to 23.5 × 8.7 and 235 × 0.87.
4 a Correct   **b** Incorrect   **c** Correct
   d Correct   **e** Incorrect   **f** Incorrect
5 a 6   **b** 0.354   **c** 21.24
   d 0.06   **e** 3.54   **f** 3540
6 B, E and F
7 Students' own three calculations that give the same answer as 6.49 × 37.2, e.g. 64.9 × 3.72, 649 × 0.372 and 0.649 × 372.
8 a 23.4 m^2 **b** £409.50

6.3 Calculations with decimals

Purposeful practice 1

1 a 4   **b** 4   **c** 40   **d** 40
2 a 3   **b** 0.3   **c** 0.3   **d** 0.03

Purposeful practice 2

1 a 900   **b** 90   **c** 9   **d** 0.9   **e** 0.09
2 a 0.09   **b** 0.9   **c** 9   **d** 90   **e** 900
3 a 7300   **b** 730   **c** 73   **d** 7.3   **e** 0.73
4 a 0.73   **b** 7.3   **c** 73   **d** 730   **e** 7300
5 a 2160   **b** 216   **c** 21.6   **d** 2.16   **e** 0.216
6 a 0.216   **b** 2.16   **c** 21.6   **d** 216   **e** 2160

Purposeful practice 3

1 a £2609.05   **b** £1713.60   **c** £1071   **d** £426.88

Problem-solving practice

1 A and F, B and I, C and J, D and G, E and H
2 a 100   **b** 0.1   **c** 31.8   **d** 0.1   **e** 100   **f** 23
3 Olivia has divided the answer to 6 ÷ 2 by 100, but dividing by 0.2 is the same as dividing by 2 and multiplying by 10, so the answer to 0.6 ÷ 0.2 is 3 × 10 × 10 = 3, not 0.03.
4 45   **5** 65.1 cm^2 **6** 32°   **7** 0.36 tonnes
8 18.625 m   **9** 0.48   **10** £127

6.4 Ratio and proportion with decimals

Purposeful practice 1

1 a £4, £24, £36   **b** £8, £20, £36   **c** £12, £16, £36
   d £8, £28, £28   **e** £16, £20, £28
2 a 8 m, 72 m, 80 m   **b** 24 m, 56 m, 80 m   **c** 16 m, 56 m, 88 m
   d 24 m, 48 m, 88 m   **e** 32 m, 40 m, 88 m
3 a 30 g, 120 g, 210 g, 390 g   **b** 60 g, 90 g, 210 g, 390 g
   c 30 g, 150 g, 180 g, 390 g   **d** 60 g, 120 g, 180 g, 390 g
   e 30 g, 120 g, 240 g, 360 g

Purposeful practice 2

1 a 1 : 2 : 3   **b** $\frac{1}{6}$ **c** $\frac{1}{3}$ **d** $\frac{1}{2}$
2 a 2 : 3 : 4   **b** $\frac{2}{9}$ **c** $\frac{1}{3}$ **d** $\frac{4}{9}$
3 a 3 : 4 : 5   **b** $\frac{1}{4}$ **c** $\frac{1}{3}$ **d** $\frac{5}{12}$
4 a 2 : 3 : 5   **b** $\frac{1}{5}$ **c** $\frac{3}{10}$ **d** $\frac{1}{2}$
5 a 1 : 2 : 4   **b** $\frac{1}{7}$ **c** $\frac{2}{7}$ **d** $\frac{4}{7}$
6 a 1 : 2 : 5   **b** $\frac{1}{8}$ **c** $\frac{1}{4}$ **d** $\frac{5}{8}$

Purposeful practice 3

1 a 4 : 7   **b** 4 : 7   **c** 4 : 7   **d** 4 : 7
   e 2 : 3   **f** 3 : 4   **g** 10 : 11   **h** 4 : 20 : 1
2 a £20, £40   **b** £15, £45   **c** £10, £50   **d** £24, £36
3 a 3.75 : 1   **b** 1 : 3.75   **c** 1 : 1.35   **d** 1.35 : 1
   e 1.37 : 1   **f** 1 : 1.37   **g** 33.67 : 1   **h** 1 : 33.67

Problem-solving practice

1 Salma is correct as she has removed the decimal and simplified. Candice has removed the decimal but not simplified. Taylor has not removed the decimal.

2 a 3.5 **b** 0.4 **c** 1.12 **d** 7.2

3 They are all correct as the ratios can be written in the form 1 : □ or □ : 1 as a decimal or fraction.

4 120g butter and 160g flour

5 £90

6

Recipe total	Flour	Butter	Sugar
800g	400g	250g	150g
1kg	0.5kg	0.3125kg	0.1875kg
2.4kg	1.2kg	0.75kg	0.45kg

7 a A 123 : 230 : 1397, B 17 : 75 : 408, C 11 : 36 : 133
b A 1 : 1.870 : 11.358; B 1 : 4.412 : 24; C 1 : 3.273 : 12.091

7 Lines and angles

7.1 Quadrilaterals

Purposeful practice 1

1 a 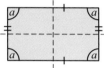 **b**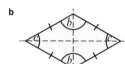

c **d**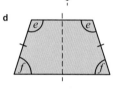

2 a Rotational symmetry of order 4 **b** Rotational symmetry of order 2

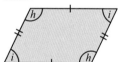

c Rotational symmetry of order 2

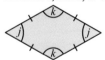

Purposeful practice 2

1 a $a = 120°$, $b = c$ **b** $a = 120°$, $b = c = 60°$
2 a $e = 110°$, $d = f$ **b** $e = 110°$, $d = f = 70°$
3 a $g = 60°$, $h = i$ **b** $g = 60°$, $h = i = 120°$
4 a $j = k$ **b** $j = k = 110°$
5 a $m = p$, $n = o$ **b** $m = p = 90°$, $n = o = 45°$
6 a $q = r$ **b** $s = 35°$, $q = r = 55°$

Problem-solving practice

1 Rectangle or rhombus
2 Rhombus, parallelogram or isosceles trapezium
3 $a = 68°$, $b = 112°$, $c = 68°$, $d = 112°$
4 The sides are all equal but not all angles; only opposite angles are equal. Also, the total of the angles is 360° and 4 × 70 = 280, not 360. $b = 70°$, but a and $c = 110°$
5 $a = 50°$, $b = 130°$, $c = 50°$, $d = 130°$
6 $a = 75°$, $b = 105°$, $c = 105°$, $d = 75°$
7 $a = 60°$, $b = 120°$

7.2 Alternate angles and proof

Purposeful practice

1 A, B, E

2 a $a = 70°$ **b** $b = 80°$ **c** $c = 120°$, $d = 60°$

3 a $e = 130°$ (angles on a straight line), $f = 50°$ (alternate angles)
b $g = 130°$ (alternate angles), $h = 50°$ (angles on a straight line)
c $j = 80°$ (angles on a straight line), $k = 80°$ (alternate angles)
d $l = 100°$ (alternate angles), $m = 80°$ (angles on a straight line)
e $n = 40°$ (alternate angles), $p = 80°$ (angles on a straight line)
f $q = 45°$ (angles on a straight line), $r = 45°$ (alternate angles), $s = 120°$ (angles on a straight line), $t = 60°$ (alternate angles), $u = 75°$ (angles on a straight line)
g $v = 75°$ (angles on a straight line), $w = 75°$ (alternate angles), $x = 40°$ (alternate angles), $y = 65°$ (angles on a straight line)
h $a = 50°$ (angles on a straight line), $b = 50°$ (alternate angles), $c = 30°$ (angles on a straight line), $d = 30°$ (alternate angles), $e = 100°$ (angles on a straight line)

Problem-solving practice

1 e and j, f and i, g and l, h and k because alternate angles are on different/alternate sides of each diagonal line and inside the parallel lines.
2 $x = 72°$ alternate angles, $y = 108°$ angles on a straight line.
3 Angles b and c are wrong. Angle c is alternate to 64° and $b = 116°$ angles on a straight line (or alternate angle to angle a).
4 Students' own diagrams, e.g.

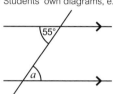

5 $x = 42°$ angles on a straight line, $y = 68°$ alternate angles, $z = 70°$ alternate angles
6 No, alternate angles lie on different sides of the diagonal but angle a is on the same side as the 130° angle.

7.3 Angles in parallel lines

Purposeful practice

1 A, B, F

2 a Angle a and 100° angle are corresponding, $a = 100°$, $b = 80°$
b Angle c and angle d are corresponding, $c = 80°$, $d = 80°$
c Angle e and angle f are corresponding, $e = 70°$, $f = 70°$
d Angle g and 120° angle are corresponding, $g = 120°$, $h = 60°$, $i = 60°$

3 a $a = 115°$ (corresponding angles), $b = 115°$ (vertically opposite angles or alternate angles), $c = 65°$ (angles on a straight line)
b $d = 60°$ (vertically opposite angles), $e = 60°$ (corresponding angles)
c $f = 140°$ (angles on a straight line), $g = 140°$ (corresponding angles), $h = 40°$ (angles on a straight line or corresponding angles), $i = 40°$ (vertically opposite angles or angles on a straight line)
d $j = 130°$ (vertically opposite angles), $k = 130°$ (corresponding angles), $l = 50°$ (angles on a straight line)
e $m = 60°$ (corresponding angles), $n = 125°$ (angles on a straight line), $p = 60°$ (vertically opposite or alternate angles), $q = 125°$ (corresponding angles)
f $r = 45°$ (alternate angles), $s = 80°$ (vertically opposite angles), $t = 55°$ (angles on a straight line), $u = 45°$ (alternate angles), $v = 55°$ (vertically opposite angles, corresponding angles or angles, on a straight line)

Problem-solving practice

1 a and i, b and j, c and k, d and l, e and m, f and n, g and p, h and q because corresponding angles are on the same (corresponding) side of the diagonal line.

2 Students' own diagram, e.g.

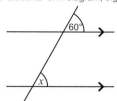

3 $a = 55°$ (vertically opposite angles),
$b = 55°$ (alternate angles or corresponding angles),
$c = 125°$ (angles on a straight line),
$d = 55°$ (corresponding angles or angles on a straight line or vertically opposite angles)

4 a True; vertically opposite angles
  b False; on a different diagonal line to each other
  c False, as $b + c$ is corresponding to j so $b + c = j$
  d True; corresponding angles
  e True; angles on a straight line
  f False; the vertically opposite angles are c and d, a and f, b and e but not d and f

5 a $a = 110°$ (corresponding angles),
    $b = 70°$ (angles on a straight line),
    $c = 70°$ (alternate angles with b),
    $d = 110°$ (corresponding angles or angles on a straight line)
  b $f = 66°$ (corresponding angles),
    $e = 114°$ (angles on a straight line),
    $g = 114°$ (opposite angles in a parallelogram are equal),
    $h = 66°$ (opposite angles in a parallelogram are equal or alternate angles with f)

6 $57°$ (given), $a = 68°$ (angles on a straight line and corresponding angles), $b = 55°$ (angles on a straight line and corresponding angles, or angles in a triangle)

7.4 Exterior and interior angles

Purposeful practice 1

1 a i $720°$ **ii** $120°$ **iii** $60°$
  b i $1080°$ **ii** $135°$ **iii** $45°$
  c i $1440°$ **ii** $144°$ **iii** $36°$
  d i $1800°$ **ii** $150°$ **iii** $30°$
2 a i $60°$ **ii** $120°$ **iii** $720°$
  b i $45°$ **ii** $135°$ **iii** $1080°$
  c i $36°$ **ii** $144°$ **iii** $1440°$
  d i $30°$ **ii** $150°$ **iii** $1800°$

Purposeful practice 2

1 a i $720°$ **ii** $a = 100°$
  b i $1080°$ **ii** $b = 130°$
  c i $900°$ **ii** $c = 160°$
  d i $1260°$ **ii** $d = 120°$

Problem-solving practice

1 $x = 86°$
2 $140° \times 8 = 1120°$ but the angle sum of an octagon $= 1080°$.
3 No, as the exterior angles of an irregular hexagon are not all the same. For a **regular** hexagon you can divide 360 by 6 to work out each exterior angle.
4 $a = 72°$, $b = 108°$, $c = 72°$, $d = 54°$
5 Hexagon
6 7
7 $x = 162°$

7.5 Solving geometric problems

Purposeful practice 1

1 a $a + 60° = 180°$ **b** $a = 120°$ **c** $60°, 120°$
2 a $2b + 60° = 180°$ **b** $b = 60°$ **c** $60°, 120°$
3 a $2c + 110° = 180°$ **b** $c = 35°$ **c** $70°, 110°$
4 a $2d + 80° = 180°$ **b** $d = 50°$ **c** $50°, 50°, 80°$
5 a $2e + 90° = 180°$ **b** $e = 45°$ **c** $45°, 45°, 90°$
6 a $3f + 90° = 180°$ **b** $f = 30°$ **c** $30°, 60°, 90°$
7 a $g + 100° = 180°$ **b** $g = 80°$ **c** $30°, 70°, 80°$
8 a $2h + 70° = 180°$ **b** $h = 55°$ **c** $55°, 55°, 70°$

9 a $5x = 180°$ **b** $x = 36°$ **c** $36°, 72°, 72°$
10 a $3y + 60° = 180°$ **b** $y = 40°$ **c** $40°, 60°, 80°$
11 a $4k + 80° = 360°$ **b** $k = 70°$ **c** $50°, 70°, 100°, 140°$
12 a $7m + 10° = 360°$ **b** $m = 50°$ **c** $50°, 70°, 110°, 130°$

Purposeful practice 2

1 $a = 140°$ **2** $b = 30°$ **3** $c = 35°$
4 $d = 18°$ **5** $e = 50°$ **6** $f = 30°$

Problem-solving practice

1 a $50°, 50°, 50°$ **b** $54°, 54°, 54°, 54°, 54°$
  c $36°, 54°$
2 a $30°, 50°, 100°$ **b** $110°, 160°$
  c $44°, 94°, 111°, 111°$
3 $40°, 60°, 80°$
4 $65°, 65°, 115°, 115°$
5 $x = 30°$
6 $y = 35°$
7 $x = 20°, y = 110°$

Mixed exercises B

Mixed problem-solving practice B

1 a $10x - 3$ **b** $x = 6$
2 a A: old, B: new, C: new, D: old
  b 2318.52 cm^2
3 a For example, $7(2x + 5) - 3 \times 4 = 14x + 35 - 12 = 14x + 23$
  b $x = 4$
4 $2x = 70°$ (corresponding angles are equal), so $x = 35°$.
    $3y + 10° = 115°$ (alternate angles are equal), so $y = 35°$.
    $x = 35°, y = 35°$
5 a i $45d + 40 = 310$
    ii $d = 6$
  b i Because the point P is plotted at $C = 310$ and shows that the correponding value of d is 6.
    ii $45d + 40 = 220$
  c $45d + 40 = 445$, $d = 9$
  d The charge per day for the car.
  e A one-off hire fee.
6 $70°, 133°, 132°, 70°, 135°$
7 Angle DAB = angle $BCD = 40°$,
    angle ABC = angle $CDA = 140°$
8 a After 25 seconds, because this is where the graph lines cross.
  b Vase B, as this curve is steeper than the curve for A in the first 10 seconds.
9 Annabel, as her meal costs about £15 and Kris's meal costs about £13.75.

8 Calculating with fractions

8.1 Ordering fractions

Purposeful practice 1

1 More than $\frac{1}{2}$: $\frac{2}{3}, \frac{3}{4}, \frac{4}{5}, \frac{4}{6}, \frac{5}{6}$
  Equal to $\frac{1}{2}$: $\frac{2}{4}, \frac{3}{6}$
  Less than $\frac{1}{2}$: $\frac{1}{3}, \frac{1}{4}, \frac{1}{5}, \frac{2}{5}, \frac{1}{6}, \frac{2}{6}$
2 A, B and D
3 a $\frac{3}{4}, \frac{1}{2}, \frac{3}{8}$ **b** $\frac{3}{4}, \frac{4}{8}, \frac{1}{4}$ **c** $\frac{5}{8}, \frac{1}{2}, \frac{1}{4}$
  d $\frac{3}{4}, \frac{1}{2}, \frac{2}{5}$ **e** $\frac{3}{5}, \frac{1}{2}, \frac{3}{10}$ **f** $\frac{5}{8}, \frac{5}{10}, \frac{2}{5}$
  g $\frac{8}{12}, \frac{6}{12}, \frac{2}{5}$ **h** $\frac{5}{6}, \frac{6}{12}, \frac{1}{5}$ **i** $\frac{7}{12}, \frac{3}{6}, \frac{1}{3}$

Purposeful practice 2

1 a $\frac{1}{2}, \frac{3}{5}, \frac{4}{5}$ **b** $\frac{1}{2}, \frac{3}{5}, \frac{7}{10}$ **c** $\frac{1}{2}, \frac{13}{20}, \frac{7}{10}$
  d $\frac{1}{2}, \frac{2}{3}, \frac{7}{10}$ **e** $\frac{1}{2}, \frac{11}{18}, \frac{2}{3}$ **f** $\frac{1}{2}, \frac{17}{30}, \frac{3}{5}$
  g $\frac{1}{2}, \frac{23}{30}, \frac{13}{15}$ **h** $\frac{1}{2}, \frac{3}{5}, \frac{11}{15}$ **i** $\frac{4}{15}, \frac{7}{20}, \frac{1}{2}$

2 a $\frac{11}{15}, \frac{2}{3}, \frac{3}{5}$ **b** $\frac{3}{4}, \frac{5}{8}, \frac{7}{16}$ **c** $\frac{7}{9}, \frac{13}{18}, \frac{2}{3}$

d $\frac{7}{10}, \frac{2}{3}, \frac{3}{5}$ **e** $\frac{4}{5}, \frac{11}{15}, \frac{7}{10}$ **f** $\frac{11}{15}, \frac{3}{5}, \frac{4}{9}$

g $\frac{5}{6}, \frac{3}{4}, \frac{4}{9}$ **h** $\frac{6}{7}, \frac{5}{6}, \frac{2}{3}$ **i** $\frac{13}{24}, \frac{7}{16}, \frac{3}{8}$

Problem-solving practice

1 A fraction 'more than $\frac{1}{2}$' is $\frac{2}{3}$ or $\frac{3}{4}$.

A fraction 'less than $\frac{1}{2}$' is $\frac{1}{4}$ or $\frac{1}{3}$.

2 a Shop C   **b** Shop B

3 No, the correct order should be $\frac{2}{5}, \frac{7}{20}, \frac{3}{10}$.

4 Green, red, blue

5 Phillip hasn't taken into account the denominators.
The correct order should be $\frac{7}{12}, \frac{4}{5}, \frac{5}{6}$.

6 Meera, Belle, Phil, Edward

7 Students' own answers showing a list of fractions in ascending
order, for example, $\frac{1}{2}, \frac{3}{5}, \frac{5}{6}, \frac{7}{8}, \frac{9}{10}$.

8.2 Adding and subtracting fractions

Purposeful practice 1

1 a $\frac{3}{4}$ **b** $\frac{3}{8}$ **c** $\frac{3}{16}$ **d** $\frac{3}{10}$

e $\frac{3}{20}$ **f** $\frac{3}{40}$ **g** $\frac{3}{14}$ **h** $\frac{3}{22}$

2 a $\frac{5}{6}$ **b** $\frac{5}{8}$ **c** $\frac{9}{14}$ **d** $\frac{7}{20}$

e $\frac{7}{9}$ **f** $\frac{8}{15}$ **g** $\frac{11}{20}$ **h** $\frac{13}{36}$

3 a $\frac{1}{2}$ **b** $\frac{1}{4}$ **c** $\frac{1}{8}$ **d** $\frac{1}{2}$

e $\frac{3}{4}$ **f** $\frac{1}{4}$ **g** $\frac{1}{4}$ **h** $\frac{5}{18}$

4 a $1\frac{1}{4}$ **b** $1\frac{1}{8}$ **c** $1\frac{1}{10}$ **d** $1\frac{1}{6}$

5 a $1\frac{1}{2}$ **b** $1\frac{1}{2}$ **c** $1\frac{1}{3}$ **d** $1\frac{1}{6}$

Purposeful practice 2

1 a $\frac{1}{4}$ **b** $\frac{1}{8}$ **c** $\frac{1}{10}$ **d** $\frac{1}{6}$

e $\frac{1}{9}$ **f** $\frac{2}{15}$ **g** $\frac{7}{16}$ **h** $\frac{7}{25}$

2 a $\frac{1}{2}$ **b** $\frac{1}{4}$ **c** $\frac{1}{4}$ **d** $\frac{3}{4}$

Purposeful practice 3

1 a $\frac{7}{12}$ **b** $\frac{9}{10}$ **c** $\frac{11}{15}$ **d** $\frac{17}{20}$

e $\frac{7}{24}$ **f** $\frac{13}{36}$ **g** $\frac{5}{6}$ **h** $\frac{5}{12}$

2 a $1\frac{1}{6}$ **b** $1\frac{1}{10}$ **c** $1\frac{1}{18}$ **d** $1\frac{5}{12}$

e $1\frac{4}{15}$ **f** $1\frac{5}{24}$ **g** $1\frac{7}{12}$ **h** $1\frac{1}{30}$

Problem-solving practice

1 $\frac{7}{10}$

2 $\frac{7}{20}$

3 a Avinash has subtracted the numerators and subtracted the
denominators instead of finding a common denominator.

b $\frac{1}{3}$

4 a $\frac{31}{40}$ **b** $\frac{9}{40}$

5 Leila hasn't converted the fractions to their equivalent fractions
correctly, as she hasn't multiplied 5 by 4 or 1 by 9 to give
$\frac{20}{36} + \frac{9}{36} = \frac{29}{36}$

6 Students' own answers of two fractions with different
denominators that total $\frac{3}{10}$, for example, $\frac{1}{5} + \frac{1}{10}$.

7 $\frac{5}{12}$

8.3 Multiplying fractions

Purposeful practice 1

1 a 16   **b** 12   **c** 8   **d** 6

2 a 32   **b** 36   **c** 40   **d** 42

e 44   **f** 45   **g** 46   **h** 47

Purposeful practice 2

1 a $\frac{1}{15}$ **b** $\frac{2}{15}$ **c** $\frac{2}{21}$ **d** $\frac{2}{35}$

2 a $\frac{1}{3}$ **b** $\frac{1}{6}$ **c** $\frac{1}{8}$ **d** $\frac{1}{12}$

e $\frac{1}{6}$ **f** $\frac{1}{6}$ **g** $\frac{3}{5}$ **h** $\frac{5}{8}$

3 a $-\frac{15}{28}$ **b** $-\frac{15}{28}$ **c** $-\frac{9}{20}$ **d** $\frac{6}{35}$

4 a $-\frac{3}{10}$ **b** $-\frac{1}{12}$ **c** $\frac{1}{6}$ **d** $\frac{2}{5}$

Purposeful practice 3

1 a $\frac{1 \times 3}{2 \times 4} = \frac{3}{8}$ **b** $\frac{1 \times 1}{6 \times 15} = \frac{1}{90}$

c $\frac{1 \times 5}{2 \times 11} = \frac{5}{22}$ **d** $\frac{1 \times 1}{4 \times 3} = \frac{1}{12}$

2 a $\frac{1}{8}$ **b** $\frac{1}{24}$ **c** $\frac{1}{8}$ **d** $\frac{1}{15}$

e $\frac{1}{24}$ **f** $\frac{1}{8}$ **g** $\frac{1}{24}$ **h** $\frac{1}{24}$

3 a $\frac{3}{40}$ **b** $\frac{2}{45}$ **c** $\frac{4}{35}$ **d** $\frac{16}{63}$

Problem-solving practice

1 a 40   **b** 150   **c** 10

2 a =   **b** >

3 72

4 $\frac{5}{9}$ m²

5 Shop B, as he saves £200 there but only £150 at shop A.

6 a $\frac{3}{7}$ **b** $-\frac{2}{5}$

7 a Grant hasn't fully simplified his answer. He should have
written $\frac{1 \times 5}{2 \times 7}$, not $\frac{4 \times 5}{8 \times 7}$

b $\frac{5}{14}$

8.4 Dividing fractions

Purposeful practice 1

1 a $\frac{2}{3}$ **b** $\frac{3}{4}$ **c** $\frac{2}{5}$ **d** $\frac{3}{5}$

e $\frac{3}{2}$ **f** $\frac{4}{3}$ **g** $\frac{5}{2}$ **h** $\frac{5}{3}$

2 a 6   **b** 7   **c** 8   **d** 9

e $\frac{1}{4}$ **f** $\frac{1}{14}$ **g** $\frac{1}{24}$ **h** $\frac{1}{108}$

Purposeful practice 2

1 a 4   **b** 6   **c** 6   **d** 9

e 12   **f** 12   **g** 16   **h** 25

2 a 60   **b** 30   **c** 20   **d** 15

e 90   **f** 45   **g** 30   **h** 18

Purposeful practice 3

1 a $\frac{2}{3}$ **b** $\frac{5}{7}$ **c** $\frac{5}{9}$ **d** $\frac{11}{13}$

e $\frac{3}{2}$ **f** $\frac{7}{5}$ **g** $\frac{9}{5}$ **h** $\frac{13}{11}$

2 a $\frac{8}{15}$ **b** $\frac{14}{15}$ **c** $\frac{8}{27}$ **d** $\frac{28}{45}$

3 a $\frac{4}{5}$ **b** $\frac{6}{7}$ **c** $\frac{3}{4}$ **d** $\frac{5}{8}$

e $\frac{11}{18}$ **f** $\frac{2}{5}$ **g** $\frac{2}{3}$ **h** $\frac{5}{6}$

4 a $1\frac{1}{15}$ **b** $1\frac{5}{28}$ **c** $1\frac{13}{27}$ **d** $1\frac{1}{9}$

Problem-solving practice

1 a $\frac{7}{3}$ **b** 1   **c** $\frac{1}{8}$ **d** 1

e A fraction or integer multiplied by its reciprocal is 1.

f Students' own answers; the result of a multiplication should
always be 1.

2 $\frac{1}{4}$ **3** 20   **4** $\frac{5}{12}$

5 Layla, as she has multiplied by the reciprocal of the divisor.
Ella has used the reciprocal of both fractions, not just the divisor.
Ebo has divided the numerators and denominators so his answer
is not properly simplified.

6 Callum is incorrect: dividing by a number greater than 1 makes what you start with smaller ($20 \div 5 = 4$), dividing by 1 gives the same number ($20 \div 1 = 20$) and dividing by a fraction less than 1 makes the number you start with bigger $\left(20 \div \frac{1}{5} = 100 \text{ and } \frac{1}{20} \div \frac{1}{5} = \frac{1}{4}\right)$.

8.5 Calculating with mixed numbers

Purposeful practice 1

1 a $3\frac{3}{5}$ **b** 4 **c** $4\frac{1}{5}$ **d** $7\frac{2}{5}$

2 a $3\frac{7}{10}$ **b** 4 **c** $4\frac{1}{2}$ **d** $7\frac{1}{2}$

3 a $3\frac{7}{20}$ **b** $3\frac{11}{20}$ **c** $4\frac{1}{20}$ **d** $7\frac{1}{20}$

Purposeful practice 2

1 a $2\frac{2}{9}$ **b** $1\frac{8}{9}$ **c** $1\frac{8}{9}$ **d** $1\frac{2}{3}$

2 a $\frac{1}{18}$ **b** $\frac{7}{18}$ **c** $\frac{11}{18}$ **d** $\frac{5}{18}$

3 a $2\frac{1}{4}$ **b** $2\frac{5}{8}$ **c** $1\frac{3}{8}$ **d** $1\frac{5}{8}$

Purposeful practice 3

1 a $2\frac{1}{6}$ **b** $8\frac{2}{3}$ **c** $10\frac{5}{6}$ **d** $10\frac{1}{2}$

   e 33 **f** $35\frac{1}{2}$ **g** 24 **h** $25\frac{5}{7}$

2 a $2\frac{1}{2}$ **b** $1\frac{1}{3}$ **c** $7\frac{1}{9}$ **d** 15

   e $1\frac{1}{2}$ **f** $2\frac{2}{9}$ **g** $3\frac{7}{11}$ **h** $\frac{11}{15}$

Problem-solving practice

1 $3\frac{7}{15}$ miles   **2** $3\frac{11}{20}$ litres   **3** $4\frac{1}{5}$ m²

4

5

×	$1\frac{1}{2}$	$2\frac{1}{4}$	$2\frac{1}{3}$
$1\frac{2}{5}$	$2\frac{1}{10}$	$3\frac{3}{20}$	$3\frac{4}{15}$
$1\frac{3}{8}$	$2\frac{1}{16}$	$3\frac{3}{32}$	$3\frac{5}{24}$
$2\frac{1}{3}$	$3\frac{1}{2}$	$5\frac{1}{4}$	$5\frac{4}{9}$

6 a Max has multiplied the whole numbers together and then the fractions together. He should have changed both mixed numbers to improper fractions and multiplied them together.

   b 4

9 Straight-line graphs

9.1 Direct proportion on graphs

Purposeful practice 1

C, F

Purposeful practice 2

1 a £2.50

   b i 600 g   **ii** 240 g   **iii** 1600 g

2 a Yes, as the graph is a single straight line through the origin.

   b No, as the graph is not a single straight line, nor through the origin. (This may be because postage and packaging are added.)

Purposeful practice 3

Students should show their own reasoning for each question. Example answers are given.

1 Yes, because when the number of feet doubles, so does the number of centimetres.

2 No, because when the hours worked multiples by 2.5, the pay multiplies by 3.125.

Problem-solving practice

1 a i £95   **ii** £220

   b 15 hours

   c No, because the graph does not go through (0, 0).

2 a 8 kg is heavier, as 8 kg ≈ 17.6 lb.

   b The dog gained weight, as 48 kg ≈ 105.6 lb. Students may also answer that it is impossible to tell given that both values could be rounded.

   c Yes, because it is a straight line graph through (0, 0).

3 Because when the number of years doubles from 3 to 6, the value does not double ($16\,000 \times 2 \neq 30\,000$).

9.2 Gradients

Purposeful practice 1

1 a

x	−2	−1	0	1	2
y	−1	0	1	2	3

b

x	−2	−1	0	1	2
y	1	2	3	4	5

c

x	−2	−1	0	1	2
y	−3	−1	1	3	5

d

x	−2	−1	0	1	2
y	−1	1	3	5	7

2

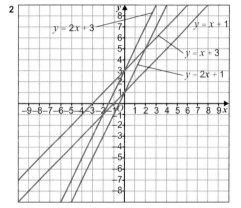

Purposeful practice 2

1 a

x	−2	−1	0	1	2
y	3	2	1	0	−1

b

x	−2	−1	0	1	2
y	5	4	3	2	1

c

x	−2	−1	0	1	2
y	5	3	1	−1	−3

d

x	−2	−1	0	1	2
y	7	5	3	1	−1

2

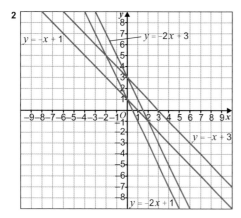

Purposeful practice 3

A: 0.5, B: 1, C: 2, D: −3, E: −1, G: 1, H: 2, I: 4, J: −4, K: −2, L: −1

Problem-solving practice

1 a The graph should be one straight line.

b

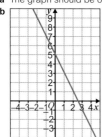

2 a i

x	−2	−1	0	1	2
y	−2	−1	0	1	2

ii

x	−2	−1	0	1	2
y	4	2	0	−2	−4

b

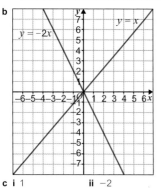

c i 1   **ii** −2

3 a Gradient 1: E, G, H; gradient 2: D, F; gradient −1: A, C; gradient −2: B

  b Students' own line with gradient −2.

4 Students' own line in each case, with gradients given in the question of 1, −1, 2, −2.

9.3 Equations of straight lines

Purposeful practice 1

1 a i

x	−2	−1	0	1	2
y	−9	−6	−3	0	3

ii

x	−2	−1	0	1	2
y	−8	−5	−2	1	4

iii

x	−2	−1	0	1	2
y	−7	−4	−1	2	5

iv

x	−2	−1	0	1	2
y	−4	−1	2	5	8

b

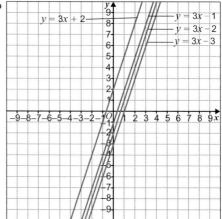

2 a i

x	−2	−1	0	1	2
y	2	1	0	−1	−2

ii

x	−2	−1	0	1	2
y	3	2	1	0	−1

iii

x	−2	−1	0	1	2
y	5	3	1	−1	−3

iv

x	−2	−1	0	1	2
y	7	4	1	−2	−5

b

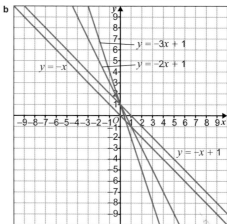

Purposeful practice 2

1 E **2** D **3** F **4** B **5** C **6** A

Problem-solving practice

1

Equation	Gradient	y-intercept
$y = x + 5$	1	5
$y = x − 5$	1	−5
$y = −2x + 3$	−2	3
$y = −3x + 2$	−3	2
$y = 4x − 5$	4	−5
$y = 5x + 2$	5	2

2 No, the 3s mean different things. The line with equation $y = 3x - 1$ has gradient 3 but the line with equation $y = x - 3$ has gradient 1 so they are not parallel.

3 No, as the line $y = 2x - 5$ has y-intercept -5 but the line $y = 2x + 5$ has y-intercept 5.

4 a Students' own four lines parallel to $y = 2x - 3$ (all with gradient 2).

b Students' own two lines with y-intercept -3.

5 a $A: y = x + 3$, $B: y = -x - 1$

b Students' lines that complete a square, for example $y = x - 1$ and $y = -x + 3$.

6 a E and G because they have the same number in front of x (3).

b A, D and F because they all contain the constant -1.

c $y = -5x + c$ where $c \neq 1$

d $y = mx - 2$ where $m \neq -3$

10 Percentages, decimals and fractions

10.1 Fractions and decimals

Purposeful practice 1

1 a 0.003   **b** 0.03 or 0.030   **c** 0.303

d 0.033   **e** 0.33 or 0.330   **f** 0.0033

g 0.0303   **h** 0.033 or 0.0330

2 a $\frac{9}{100}$ **b** $\frac{9}{1000}$ **c** $\frac{9}{10\,000}$

d $\frac{99}{1000}$ **e** $\frac{99}{10\,000}$ **f** $\frac{999}{10\,000}$

3 a $\frac{1}{25}$ **b** $\frac{1}{250}$ **c** $\frac{1}{2500}$

d $\frac{11}{250}$ **e** $\frac{11}{2500}$ **f** $\frac{111}{2500}$

Purposeful practice 2

1 a 0.0625   **b** 0.125   **c** 0.1875   **d** 0.25

e 0.3125   **f** 0.375   **g** 0.4375   **h** 0.5

2 a $0.\dot{3}$ **b** $0.\dot{6}$ **c** $0.0\dot{9}$ **d** $0.1\dot{8}$

e $0.2\dot{7}$ **f** $0.3\dot{6}$ **g** $0.4\dot{5}$ **h** $0.5\dot{4}$

Purposeful practice 3

1 a 2.05   **b** 2.1   **c** 2.15   **d** 2.2

e 2.25   **f** 2.3

2 a $2.0\dot{3}$ **b** $2.0\dot{6}$ **c** $2.1\dot{3}$

Problem-solving practice

1 a False, as for 0.0007, the digit 7 is in the ten thousandths column, not the thousandths column.

b True, as 2 is in the ten thousandths column.

c True, as $0.006 = \frac{6}{1000}$ which simplifies to $\frac{3}{500}$

2 a Terminating: $\frac{1}{2}, \frac{1}{4}, \frac{1}{5}, \frac{1}{8}, \frac{1}{10}$; recurring: $\frac{1}{3}, \frac{1}{6}, \frac{1}{7}, \frac{1}{9}, \frac{1}{11}, \frac{1}{12}$

b If the only prime factors of its denominator are 2 and/or 5, then a fraction will be written as a terminating decimal.
If the denominator has other prime factors, then the fraction will be written as a recurring decimal.

3 a i $\frac{1}{125}$ **ii** $\frac{1}{200}$

b i 0.008   **ii** 0.005

4 No, $\frac{1}{3} = 0.\dot{3}$, not 0.3

5 a $0.55 = \frac{55}{100}$ but 55 minutes $= \frac{55}{60}$ so 0.55 is not equal to 55 minutes.

b 33 minutes

6 Terminating decimals: A, D, E. Recurring decimals: B, C, F. For terminating decimals, still the minutes are a multiple of 3; for recurring decimals, the minutes aren't a multiple of 3.

7 Dan, as Dan spends 1 hour 45 minutes, Lucy spends 1 hour 44 minutes, Abdul spends 1 hour 42 minutes.

10.2 Equivalent proportions

Purposeful practice 1

1 a 0.2   **b** 1.2   **c** 27.2   **d** 27.6

e 0.04   **f** 32.04   **g** 32.08   **h** 32.16

2 a 20%   **b** 120%   **c** 4%   **d** 104%

e 204%   **f** 216%   **g** 205%   **h** 215%

3 a $1\frac{1}{10}$ **b** $1\frac{3}{10}$ **c** $1\frac{7}{10}$ **d** $2\frac{7}{10}$

e $1\frac{1}{20}$ **f** $1\frac{3}{4}$ **g** $1\frac{7}{20}$ **h** $2\frac{7}{20}$

i $1\frac{1}{50}$ **j** $1\frac{7}{50}$

Purposeful practice 2

1 a 0.025, 2.5%   **b** 0.05, 5%   **c** 0.075, 7.5%

d 0.1, 10%   **e** 0.125, 12.5%   **f** 0.15, 15%

g 0.175, 17.5%   **h** 0.2, 20%

2 a 0.008, 0.8%   **b** 0.016, 1.6%   **c** 0.024, 2.4%

d 0.012, 1.2%   **e** 0.016, 1.6%   **f** 0.02, 2%

g 0.012, 1.2%   **h** 0.014, 1.4%

3 a 1%   **b** 0.5%   **c** 1.5%   **d** 15%   **e** 45%

Purposeful practice 3

1 a 1.25   **b** 2.25   **c** 2.5   **d** 12.5

2 a $0.021, \frac{21}{1000}$ **b** $0.042, \frac{21}{500}$ **c** $0.084, \frac{21}{250}$

d $0.105, \frac{21}{200}$ **e** $0.375, \frac{3}{8}$ **f** $0.625, \frac{5}{8}$

g $0.875, \frac{7}{8}$

Problem-solving practice

1 No, as $\frac{1}{2} = 50\%$ and $3 = 300\%$, so $3\frac{1}{2} = 350\%$

2 C (25.1)

3 $2\frac{3}{5} = 260\%$, so 255% is smaller.

4 Seth achieves the highest mark as Seth scores $\frac{54}{80} = \frac{27}{40} = 67.5\%$, Katie scores $\frac{5}{8} = 62.5\%$ and Esme scores 65%.

5 a 64.4%   **b** Test B

6 234.5%, 23.45, $23\frac{4}{5}$

7 a 1.75   **b** $1\frac{3}{4}$ **c** $115\% = 1.15 = 1\frac{15}{100} = 1\frac{3}{20}$

10.3 Writing percentages

Purposeful practice 1

1 a 50%   **b** 25%   **c** 10%   **d** 35%

e 70%   **f** 24%   **g** 48%   **h** 34%

2 a 25%   **b** 12.5%   **c** 37.5%   **d** 75%

e 30%   **f** 60%   **g** 120%   **h** 240%

3 a 25%   **b** 26%   **c** 13%   **d** 10.4%

e 11%   **f** 22%   **g** 44%   **h** 110%

Purposeful practice 2

1 a £12   **b** £24   **c** £36   **d** £48

e £14.40   **f** £28.80   **g** £43.20   **h** £57.60

2 a i 60g   **ii** 540g   **b i** 30g   **ii** 270g

c i 15g   **ii** 135g   **d i** 7.5g   **ii** 67.5g

3 a i 30g   **ii** 570g   **iii** 90g   **iv** 510g

b i 15g   **ii** 285g   **iii** 45g   **iv** 255g

c i 7.5g   **ii** 142.5g   **iii** 22.5g   **iv** 127.5g

d i 3.75g   **ii** 71.25g   **iii** 11.25g   **iv** 63.75g

Purposeful practice 3

1 a i £50 500   **ii** £51 000   **b i** £5050   **ii** £5100

c i £505   **ii** £510   **d i** £50.50   **ii** £51

2 a i £50 250   **ii** £50 500   **b i** £5025   **ii** £5050

c i £502.50   **ii** £505   **d i** £50.25   **ii** £50.50

Problem-solving practice

1 a 10%   **b** 12%

2 William is correct, as Eva divides by 400 but the total amount of drink is 500 ml.

3 a 1380   **b** 1455

4 £10 800

5 £1680

6 10% of £30 = £3, so the discount is £3 per shirt, so the discount for two shirts is £6, which is still 10% of the total price.
20% of £60 = £12 which is double £6, so Laura is incorrect.

7 Option A, as 1.5% of £3000 for 10 years is £450 but for option B 12% of £3000 = £360.

10.4 Percentages of amounts

Purposeful practice 1

1 a 0.8 **b** 0.08 **c** 1.8 **d** 1.08
2 a 1.1 **b** 1.11 **c** 1.01 **d** 2
3 a 0.5 **b** 0.45 **c** 0.95 **d** 0.55 **e** 0.05

Purposeful practice 2

1 a £77 **b** £84 **c** £91 **d** £105
  e 440 g **f** 480 g **g** 520 g **h** 600 g
2 a $54 **b** $6 **c** $48 **d** $12
  e 180 ml **f** 20 ml **g** 160 ml **h** 40 ml

Purposeful practice 3

1 a 3000 km **b** 1500 km **c** 1000 km
  d 750 km **e** 375 km **f** 200 km
2 a 1200 litres **b** 800 litres **c** 400 litres
  d 300 litres **e** 200 litres **f** 20 litres

Problem-solving practice

1 No, as 6% = 0.06, not 0.6, so he should have written
  92 × 0.06 = £5.52
2 A and E, B and H, C and F, D and G
3 Shop B as it costs £960 from shop A and £825 from shop B.
4 No, as the phone costs £357.
5 675 **6** £450 **7** £120

Mixed exercises C

Mixed problem-solving practice C

1 Ellen, Arif, Leon
2 $\frac{7}{8}$ because $\frac{4}{5} = \frac{96}{120}$, $\frac{7}{8} = \frac{105}{120}$, $\frac{2}{3} = \frac{80}{120}$ and 96 is closer to 105 than to 80.
3 a $\frac{1}{2}$ **b** $\frac{29}{60}$
4 69 boxes **5** 14 375 m^2 **6** 22.5%
7 a $10\frac{1}{4}$ inches **b** $6\frac{3}{32}$ inches^2
8 a $1\frac{7}{30}$ **b** $\frac{11}{20}$ **c** $\frac{7}{12}$ **d** $\frac{1}{30}$ **e** $\frac{1}{3}$ **f** $\frac{3}{40}$
9

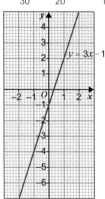

10 3 of Box 2 as this costs £12.75, but 5 of Box 1 costs £14
11 20
12 a Fixed charge per day
  b Cost of each kilowatt hour
  c $y = 16x + 14$ (students might use different letters for the variables)
  d No, as the graph does not go through the origin.
13 5 years

14 a

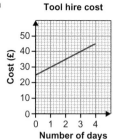

Tool hire cost

b $y = 5x + 25$ (students might use different letters for the variables)
15 Yes, as total expenses £193 600, wages £102 900, rent £10 500, other expenses £4000;
  193 600 − 102 900 − 10 500 − 4000 = 76 200, which is more than 75 000.

Index